The Weird South

THE WEIRD SOUTH

Ecologies of Unknowing
in Postplantation Literature

MELANIE BENSON TAYLOR

Mercer University Lamar Memorial Lectures No. 61

THE UNIVERSITY OF GEORGIA PRESS   Athens

© 2025 by the University of Georgia Press
Athens, Georgia 30602
www.ugapress.org
All rights reserved
Set in 10/14 Sabon LT Pro
by Rebecca A. Norton

Most University of Georgia Press titles are
available from popular e-book vendors.

Printed digitally

EU Authorized Representative
Easy Access System Europe—Mustamäe tee 50, 10621
Tallinn, Estonia, gpsr.requests@easproject.com

Library of Congress Cataloging-in-Publication Data

Names: Taylor, Melanie Benson, 1976– author.
Title: The weird South : ecologies of unknowing in postplantation literature /
Melanie Benson Taylor.
Description: Athens : The University of Georgia Press, 2025. |
Series: Mercer University Lamar Memorial Lectures; no. 61 |
Includes bibliographical references and index.
Identifiers: LCCN 2025007422 | ISBN 9780820373836 (hardback) |
ISBN 9780820373843 (paperback) | ISBN 9780820373850 (epub) |
ISBN 9780820373867 (pdf)
Subjects: LCSH: American literature—Southern States—History and criticism. |
American literature—20th century—History and criticism. |
Landscapes in literature. | Environmental degradation in literature. |
Literature and society—United States—History—20th century. | Ecocriticism.
Classification: LCC PS261.T39 2025 | DDC 810.9975—dc23/eng/20250305
LC record available at https://lccn.loc.gov/2025007422

For Alan, Abel, and Hayden—
and especially for Amos:
we wrote this one together, you and me.

In the spring when you
come down hungry from
that other mountain
the space between one rib
and the next deep enough
to lay my finger —
how much of you will
remain or linger —
bone or mouth or memory
of the first sadness of humans?
Will you dig from the crevices
the paper where they
wrote you down as *this*
instead of *that?* Or startle
at the clatter of plates?
The creak of the wooden bed?
Will your skin shake off
its fur, your claws remember
they were fingers? And the hands,
meaty as paws, soften into
what I once could stroke or suckle?

—*FROM JANET MCADAMS, "HUNTERS, GATHERERS"*
POETRY (JUNE 2018)

Contents

Foreword, by Douglas E. Thompson   *xi*

Preface   *xv*

Acknowledgments   *xix*

CHAPTER 1.
The Grave
1

CHAPTER 2.
The Trees
31

CHAPTER 3.
The Forest
61

Notes   *85*

Index   *95*

Foreword

In October 2022, Melanie Benson Taylor addressed the Mercer University and Macon communities through the Eugenia Dorothy Blount Lamar Memorial Lectures. The "Weird" South has had many meanings over the past two hundred years. In this series of lectures, however, the "web" of weirdness extends out, in, and down as a haunting of the landscape we identify with the southern part of the United States. But in this case, the weirdness isn't something unique about the South but how "entangled" the region is with every aspect of the landscape. We so want to be different from creation, but every reforested cemetery or nature-consumed building reveals how little we matter. Rather than couching this in a sad light, these lectures challenge us to think about the ways that fiction writers have grappled with the overwhelming complexity of humans and nonhuman others in relationship with one another and testify to the power of narratives to see into and past those webs of particularity as we come to understand the effect of the Anthropocene and its effects on the land. Dr. Taylor moves hearers first, and readers now, through the complicated nature of the interaction between the land and the people as we become aware of the catastrophic possibility that climate change will reap on the land and us.

In a powerful reminder of how much damage exists, as we made final arrangements for the presentation of these lectures, Hurricane Ian had formed in the Atlantic Ocean and Macon had been in the cone of uncertainty for several days as we sent messages back and forth between Georgia and

xi

New Hampshire. Ian became a Category 5 hurricane in the Atlantic and after dropping in intensity over the Caribbean Sea intensified back to a Category 5 as it approached the southwest coast of Florida. It was the third costliest hurricane worldwide and left its mark on Florida from Naples across the state to Daytona and once back out in Atlantic built speed as it slammed into the Carolinas' coasts. The effects of climate change and the growing power of natural disasters suggests we have a long road ahead. Dr. Taylor's lectures weave through the landscape not as fixed or certain but as shifting and contested. Weirdness does not describe the tropes of the American South as much as the "twisted" nature of the region and its past. The lectures do not repeat mantras about the mythic South, but they are filled with engaging scholarship in southern studies that will expand what we mean when there are many Souths.

In the mid-1950s, Eugenia Dorothy Blount Lamar made a bequest to Mercer University, located in her hometown of Macon, Georgia, "to provide lectures of the very highest scholarship which will aid in the permanent preservation of the values of Southern culture, history, and literature." For sixty-five years, the Lamar Memorial Lectures committee has brought to Mercer the best minds who have examined and explained the peculiar politics, social customs, religious piety, and racial dynamics of the American South. In that time, scholars of history and literature have revealed the complexity of the region, perhaps sometimes even in contrast to Lamar's own understanding of the "permanent preservation of the values of Southern culture." Taylor treated the committee, Mercer's undergraduates, and the wider Macon community to a series of lectures that reminded us of how central the theme of apocalypse has been to the region.

Mercer University, under the work of Dr. Sarah E. Gardner, earned a National Endowment of the Humanities (NEH) Challenge grant that would over the course of five years establish a $2 million endowment to underwrite the extensive programming around southern studies at the

xii Foreword

university, including the Lamar Memorial Lecture Series. In 2017, Mercer established the Spencer B. King, Jr. Center for Southern Studies to house both the endowment and southern studies programs, with Dr. Gardner as the first director of the King Center for Southern Studies. Named after a longtime history department faculty member, the King Center for Southern Studies fosters critical discussions about the many meanings of the South. As the only center for southern studies in the United States dedicated to the education and enrichment of undergraduate students, the center's primary purpose is to examine the region's complex history and culture through courses, conversations, and events that are open, honest, and accessible.

To pull off both the lectures and the manuscript publication, the committee would like to thank two people in particular. William Altman coordinated all our efforts to bring this lecture series to Macon. Beth Snead guided the publication process as the initial three lectures turned into this book publication. I am particularly grateful to Beth for her patience and keen sense of how these published lectures help reorient the way we think and write about the American South moving forward.

With this publication, the Lamar Memorial Lectures committee would like to acknowledge six decades of work by dedicated faculty and administrators at Mercer University to sustain this valuable series to the field of southern studies. Their constant attention to bring "the very highest scholarship" to publication is a testament to the importance of critical analysis of the region and the role it plays in the nation.

Douglas E. Thompson, Chair

LAMAR MEMORIAL LECTURE COMMITTEE

DIRECTOR, SPENCER B. KING JR.,

CENTER FOR SOUTHERN STUDIES

Foreword xiii

Preface

O Man, to whatever country you belong and whatever your opinions, listen: here is your history as I believe I have read it, not in the books of your fellow men who are liars, but in Nature which never lies.

—*Jean-Jacques Rousseau*
A DISCOURSE ON INEQUALITY

When, in the spring of 2017, I received the invitation to deliver the 2022 Lamar Lectures, I was approximately twelve weeks pregnant with our second son, Hayden. All I could imagine was that by the time I traveled to Mercer University to take the podium for one of the greatest honors of my scholarly life, the unborn child inside me would be nearly five years old—and our firstborn nearly eight. What I didn't anticipate in any of my wildest imaginings was that when I delivered the lecture series in the fall of 2022, I would again be twelve weeks along, this time with our third, miraculous child, Amos.

It wasn't mystical, exactly, but it felt profoundly meaningful. I had already planned my lectures to focus on the concept of the "Weird"—an idea elaborated by theorist Timothy Morton, which he draws from "the weight of its etymological resonance from Old Norse, *urth*, which means *twist* or *turn*, as in *a twist of fate* or *a funny turn*."[1] This last pregnancy was a twist of fate indeed, and a funny turn—I was forty-five and not expecting that any more children were in our future. But more than that, Morton's use of the concept conjures the vast interconnectedness of all things—natural, human, biotic, object—that takes our current dalliance with posthumanism to a startling new level of symbiotic revelation. Morton's "weird" is like a Möbius strip, which suggests that our reality

xv

and everything it holds is a strange loop with no beginning or end, a seamless integration of disparate parts that neither invites nor allows exit or even disambiguation. As a concept in the burgeoning conversation about Anthropocenic disaster and climate emergency, the weird is a powerful way to conceptualize not just human hubris but also humility: we are no different from, no more powerful than, any other living or inanimate objects—not the organisms that take up residence in our bodies or the myriad things we think we create, fashion, patrol, and control.

By the time I began writing these lectures, the COVID-19 pandemic had already sent out an explosive signal of the porousness and vulnerability of our human bodies. Another record wildfire season on the west coast simultaneously signaled both the catastrophe of human-driven climate change and our utter powerlessness to intervene in its ravages. Conceiving and growing another human life in my own body—already one of the most mind-blowing of biological phenomena— was yet another, powerfully intimate reminder of how vitally imbricated, and how precious and precarious, the shared physical spaces of our contingent bodies can be. All of this made the writing of the "Weird South" lectures, in a blistering period of first-trimester fatigue and nausea alongside voluminous department chair duties at my home institution, a matter of strange compulsion and urgency. More than ever before in my decades of critical writing, *this* felt like messaging that could matter. How do we move forward, beyond the devastations of a brutal global pandemic, of rampant and erratic natural disasters, of explosive racial violence and police brutality? How do we take care of one another like family, and continue to honor and nurture our biotic entanglements, when everything we have done and continue to do as humans blows us steadily apart? What does it mean to recognize and honor these connections, and how do we do so in particularly haunted sites like the postplantation South?

The lectures captured my colliding sense of horror and hope. There seemed to be no way out of the agony we have

xvi Preface

created, and yet there had to be a miraculous sense of the impossible and the unthought in order to keep moving forward. What I hoped to capture and critique was the contrapuntal movement I was seeing in so much environmental, Indigenous, and southern studies conversations: efforts to both diagnose the ills of a world that only humans could create through the corrosive mechanisms and hungers of power and propriation and, at the same time, to pose fantasies of deliverance that can only be described, after all this, as delusions born of human desperation. How, I kept asking, could the same humans who wreaked so much havoc ultimately emerge from the maelstrom to be the angels of repair? Who and what can escape from the weird entanglements of the Möbius-like web of organic life, and especially of modernity and late capitalism? How can we ever hope to elevate beyond the terrors and the things we have created when they are part and parcel of us—and us of them?

These questions have application and urgency in every contemporary human context, both nationally and globally, to be sure. But they have particular resonance in the southern context, where settler-colonial, racial-capitalist, chattel-slave and agrilogistical economies have driven and produced perdurable fabrications of meaning, of identity, of difference, and of obliteration. The work of represencing, repopulating, and revising the narratives that have extracted, exploited, buried, and denied so much from so many is imposing, if not impossible. Yet the texts issuing from these contexts keen insurgently—weirdly—toward strange admissions and indomitable hopes for humanity that rest in reconstituting loss, in undoing the structures of silence and surrender, and in sussing out the vibrant collocations between the organisms and the matter that have been held fearfully apart or collapsed violently together. Some of these movements are doomed from the start, too steeped in romanticism or wish fulfillment; some are aching with the insatiable hungers and desires produced by vast, deep economies of deprivation and lack, a phenomenon that no worldly sustenance can address. The challenge

Preface xvii

of mediating these divergent glimpses into the weirdness of the postplantation, posthuman South lay in not succumbing to either fatalism or fatal hope. The mood of what follows is, therefore, necessarily dialectical, halting, ambivalent, aspirational, and cautionary.

While I'm not sure there's a clear thesis to be extracted from the movement throughout these chapters and the texts they engage, there is a poetics and a politics of witness that I hope emerges with clarity and force. There are no easy answers or solutions here because there simply are no facile fixes for the Anthropocenic crises we have engineered and let loose in the world. Our best hope, in the end, is listening to the small moments and the incipient new beginnings—the novel windows, stories, and lives being created, protected, and born each day—because these are futures quietly stealing their way into the loop. There is no way to remove ourselves from the dark histories that have made us, and that have steeped and stained our landscapes and regions and communities. Perhaps, though, we can slowly, incrementally, implosively reimagine the worlds we have made and the ones we have yet to encounter. The whole process involves a bracing humility and a surrender to the unthought and the unexpected that lies in wait on every page, in every body, in every story.

xviii Preface

Acknowledgments

Acknowledgments sections always prompt a pause of anxiety on my part, because I'm sure in advance that I will forget someone; and I know, in retrospect, that I always do. So, for that reason, I left the writing of these acknowledgements until the final moments of copyediting (bonus: I get to thank my excellent editing team!); and still, I enter into them with the humility that whatever I write with be both incomplete and inadequate.

This sentiment is not irrelevant to the subject of these pages, in fact: everything that I write about here acknowledges the inherent imbrication of the sundry subjects, objects, and forces that comprise who and what we are, say, and do. It's a futile task to untangle one's voice and agency from the conditions and the people who make any act of expression possible (or, at times, prohibitive), so this space feels like an opportunity to both bear witness and pay homage to the enlivening and enabling among those energies. This particular constellation of seed thoughts and efforts at articulation is in some ways a miracle of happenstance and privilege; it is energizing to participate in such possibility, but also chastening to recognize its paltriness. While I'll stop short of thanking Buddha and the birch trees, then, I do want to offer a blanket recognition that this book, and the words that fill it, is just a flicker among the vast network of narratives waiting to be told and straining to speak, through me, and through all of us. Which is all, I know, a bit weird . . .

With that, I want to thank all of those who not only put

xix

up with but actively encourage my (liaisons with) weirdness. First thanks, of course, go to the Mercer University hosts who invited, coordinated, prepared for, and graciously tended me before, during, and after my stay there to deliver the storied Lamar Lectures in the fall of 2022: in particular, old friends David Davis and Sarah Gardner and new friends Doug Thompson and William Aultman, all of whom shuttled me to and from hotels and airport shuttles (at truly ungodly hours—thank you, William!—so I could minimize my time away from my class and my kids); to excellent *al fresco* meals, perfect for a pregnant and pandemic-weary guest; on tours, especially one past a tremendous mansion where both Tennessee Williams and Carson McCullers once sojourned (at different times, alas), and all around and up the Ocmulgee Indian Mounds (where I met a lovely woman working in the information center, who originally and coincidentally came from my exact neck of the woods in New Hampshire / Vermont. Wonderfully weird indeed!). Most of all, the students and community members who attended my lectures were among the most rapt, generous, and lively audiences I've had the privilege of interacting with, even hours deep into my serialized droning. It will forever be an honor and a highlight of my career to have delivered these lectures and to have done so in such warm and rewarding company.

Back home, I always need to thank the people who both knew and didn't know that they were facilitating such an adventure, in the weeks leading up to the trip (when I may have missed a meeting or two) and long before that. My inimitable colleagues in both the Native American and Indigenous Studies and the English and Creative Writing departments perennially provide context, direction, and provocation to do the kind of thinking and writing I do; I am grateful for you all, and inspired by the Venn diagrams of our diverse but cocreative enthusiasms. The administration—both the people (Elizabeth Smith, Sam Levey, Matt Delmont, among others)—and the walls and tower themselves provided the architecture of space, privilege, and opportunity to write

xx   Acknowledgments

books about weird things. Working in academia at all, and especially at a place like Dartmouth, hardly qualifies as "work": I am fortunate enough to do my favorite things all day, every day, and mostly on my time and terms (or my kids'—both my own and those on loan to me in four-year cycles).

After their debut in Macon, these somewhat feral lectures languished on my laptop for over a year (while I labored to acquaint a different, human freshling into the world). I had high hopes of returning to revise my feverish ramblings into something more suited for scholarly publication; but once I mustered the time and courage to begin, I realized my ambitions made little sense: these excursions are themselves artifacts of witness, and they enact the very subject they attempt to capture. Partial and pregnant, they are seed thoughts and cracked openings that stand on their own in some ways as eruptive, disruptive invitations to further thought; to go further here would be to write another book altogether (which, gravitationally, I'm not sure I can help doing—another day). So I polished a messy piece of pottery, as it were, in hopes it will be a vessel to hold future thinking and, above all, to hold together the bits of raw material and the voices that needed such a home. Beth Snead was, as always, an eminently patient and positive guide throughout the entire process, as was the entire editorial team at Georgia Press and beyond: in particular, Jon Davies, Cristina Cotter, and Kevin Gallin (who gallantly disentangled my Möbius-like prose, provided pauses in my breathlessness, and made miraculously clear sentences out of it all). At the eleventh hour, Chris Dodge swooped in to assist with indexing and proofing the final copy; I am ever grateful for his generosity of time and expertise.

Finally, my most fulsome gratitude must go to the dear ones who have always known that I am both wordy and weird, and keep me anyway: my limitlessly giving parents, Kim and Terry; my beautiful older sister, Hiya (she has a real name, but this one makes her mine); my treasured in-

Acknowledgments xxi

laws, Diane and Robert Taylor. We span from North to South and back again, and the interleaves between us always amaze me. Lastly, my own little family has shown me exactly what weirdness really is (and I mean that in the best, most awe-struck way): my husband, Alan, who reminds me daily of the sacredness of being both singular and stitched inextricably; and, along with us, our three little boys—Abel, Hayden, and Amos—whose everyday enchantment with the unknown, the unseen, and the unexpressed are the well from which I work and survive. You four are my archive and anchor, always.

The Weird South

CHAPTER 1

The Grave

In Katherine Anne Porter's 1934 short story "The Grave," a young girl named Miranda Gay and her older brother Paul are exploring the family cemetery on their soon-to-be-sold land in West Texas. They encounter two primal, signifying discoveries: shimmering treasures from the empty grave that once contained their grandfather's remains; and, shortly thereafter, the bloated, pregnant belly of a rabbit that Paul has expertly shot and skinned. Paul buries the rabbit, with her aborted babies reinterred in her silenced womb, and commands Miranda to protect their secret. She does—even from herself, apparently, for "nearly twenty years."[1]

The story is so short that it is practically a vignette, but hammered densely into its brief frame and disturbing juxtapositions is a stunning panorama of suppressed but unrestful histories, haunting exhumations and reburials, and the mobile, ungovernable shocks of recognition and elemental truths both hidden and laid bare. All of these may be born from U.S. southern contexts, but they exceed geographical tenancy. In fact, they are more legible in remove, in periphery, in diaspora, in deferral and juxtaposition, and especially in contexts that implicate the other-than-human world as repositories and refractions of Anthropocenic catastrophe.

1

Collapsed together, they forge evocations of what I am calling the "Weird South."

For seasoned readers of southern literature, that title might first conjure up the region's and the genre's plentiful themes of peculiarity, of aberrance, of grotesquerie. The snake handlers, the deranged, the deformed, the spectacular, and the monstrous pervade the work of southern literature's most beloved writers, from Flannery O'Connor and William Faulkner to Barry Hannah and Harry Crews. To be sure, there are enough perverse subjects and themes in southern fiction to perpetuate misconceptions about not just the South's difference but its deviance.[2] I am not talking about, or implicitly endorsing, outdated views of the South as inherently backward, flawed, ignorant, or inferior. These stereotypes have long been demystified as damaging, motivated tropes that have allowed other regions and national subcultures to scapegoat the South by contrast. I am instead identifying a weirdness that exceeds both our presumptions and the region itself, subjects and themes that direct us with urgency to places and peoples that function as incubators of historical trauma.[3] These moments of weirdness, then, appear not as discrete or idiosyncratic sites or origins but as iterative, reiterative, and generative phenomena that point to an underlying ontological connectedness we have yet to fully realize or embrace.

Indeed, "weirdness" as a descriptor of either regional or literary culture far exceeds the southern context. It calls up subgenres such as the "Weird Fiction" associated with H. G. Wells and other writers of the supernatural and the speculative—perhaps best described by H. P. Lovecraft as a dramatization of the "malign suspension of the laws of nature, of the very things that we rely on to safeguard our fragile lives and psyches against the chaos and malignancy lurking just beyond the world we know."[4] Graham Harman, a major figure in the new materialism movement and particularly object-oriented ontology (ooo)—theoretical shifts that have challenged the Anthropocenic biases of contemporary continental philosophy—has championed Lovecraft's own fiction in particular,

2 *The Weird South*

and the speculative genre generally, for its version of what he calls "Weird Realism": depictions of monstrosities that are so utterly nonhuman, so beyond our cognitive capacities to assimilate, that they stun us into a dramatic consciousness of reality beyond our anthropomorphic tyrannies of knowing. Other new materialist or posthuman proponents struggle to deliver an ethics of action in response to this anticorrelationist shift. There is, they argue, a forcible unyoking of "being" (writ large) from thought (primarily human cognition), which is the reigning ontology of modernity, and in general we fail to transcend this prism. Instead, we remain detained within the matrix of human-centered logics—how do we unyoke what we think we know from the mind that knows it? Alternately, these theorists may lean too far into a fetishization of the unseen, the unknown, the unthought, and therefore into a romance of the nonhuman and object world, a recognizable reflex by which ethical humans often try to rescue subjugated others from the clutches of imperialistic human functions. This works (at least symbolically) to redress the evils of colonialism but perhaps not to elevate the once-invisible agency of the bugs, worms, and viruses that share our planet and our bodies.

But this is not exactly the kind of weird I want to explore. The Weird South I'm introducing in these pages borrows from the above traditions—of ontological reworkings and reorientations—but also revises, contradicts, upends, and expands them in ways alternately unnerving, procreative, and, finally, consciousness altering. This weirdness is not just an artistic or representational strategy, and there are typically no explicit ghosts or demons or tentacles to point to as the signifiers of all we have wreaked or tried not to see. Rather, it is a phenomenon that invites a more arresting way of understanding and responding to an unsettling reality about our sublime interconnectedness despite—or perhaps because of—our relentless impulse to cleave and separate and dominate. My southern twist on the concept of existential and ontological weirdness originates from the thinking of literary and cultural critic

The Grave 3

Timothy Morton. In his *Dark Ecology* (2016) and elsewhere, he figures the weird as a way of conceptualizing our human embeddedness in a vast biosphere of nonhuman others that both contains and erases us, an uncanny awareness that is at once desperately dark and oddly enlivening. Drawing on the Norse origins for weird meaning "twisted," or "in a loop," Morton suggests that to exist "means to be a loop, a twisted loop, like a Möbius strip . . . a non-orientable surface [where] every attempt to locate the twist on some precise region of the loop is impossible: there is no part of the surface that is not already twisted." For Morton, this is "the same as saying that reality does not come with a dotted line and a picture of scissors saying 'Cut Here,' to separate . . . its components like a good butcher (Phaedrus). Butchering reality becomes impossible."[5] This kind of thinking is essential for ecological awareness, because it allows us to see moments when "two levels that appear utterly separate flip into one another."[6] In other words, this is a weird that does not allow for human extrication or escape; this is a reality we must lean into together in order to survive it.

This is a subtle but significant shift, I think, from the new materialisms and the posthumanisms I was just summarizing. Its difference is its expansiveness, one fundamentally incompatible with the identity-rooted logics that allow us to include and exclude selectively and that prevent us from seeing our true positionality in the biosphere and our responsibilities to it and to one another. There is on the one hand inherently more functional humility, as we have to admit that there are elements of our shared existence that we can't know, a state that extends fundamentally to ourselves, caught in the loop. Here, we're all suspended in an uncanny state of partial awareness, permeated by a metaphysics of simultaneous presence and absence, here and not-here, past and futurity, a "nowness" in which we're stuck. We can no longer imagine ourselves as discrete, as contained or interpellated in any authoritative way. Rather, we become a dynamic being in kinetic co-constitution with other humans, animals, nonhumans, objects, viruses—a landscape of being where all things are "actors," and "[r]eality, in the end, is a kind of drama."[7] What more potent way of invoking the undeadness of southern histories, the mobilizing power of its narratives, and our stunned incapacity either to fully grasp or to remove ourselves from any of it?

Indeed, to my mind, Morton's concept finds its richest applications—as well as its most ponderous challenges—in a context like that of the postplantation U.S. South. Here is Lovecraftian weirdness with a gentle inversion: instead of a "suspension" of the laws of nature, the southern context more often than not exposes in its very material structures and psychological enmeshments the inherent chaos and malignancy, and perhaps eventually the revelatory power and grace, of the tangled world of human, nature, animal, object, *fill-in-the-blank*-other that simultaneously resists and submits to human organization, where its marks are everywhere and nowhere, exposed and obscured. It is the dialectical work of the weird southern text to manifest and conceal all at once. Rather than slip into reverse hierarchies, or empty redemptions, or reflexive denunciations of Anthropocenic catastrophe—indeed, instead of sidelining human agency—it seems to demand more: more witness, more consciousness, more action, more repair. The weirdness of the postplantation is the kind made possible only by a deep acknowledgment of human hubris rather than a pantomime of humility, even as it redoubles our confrontation with all that societies structured by settler colonialism and racial capitalism have irrevocably wrought. This is an ethics both motivated and made possible by perhaps the most critical emergency of our times, that of ecological apocalypse and climate disaster, the human-driven wreckage of our earth, and especially our reckoning with the furious bundle of economic, racial, and imperial etiologies at the epicenter of that ruin where power structures both determine and dissolve clear markers of complicity or victimhood. So much trauma and destruction is brought to consciousness that we can't look at it head-on but only in partial glimpses

The Grave 5

and textual elisions, in silence and subtlety, in the spectral forms whose haunting afterlives are assured.

The challenge here, of course, is not giving up. Not retreating into the despair of the late Anthropocene, where we recognize that since humans have destroyed everything, we have no portal to salvation unless we resign ourselves to disappearance, to inconsequentiality, to powerlessness—"learning to die," as Roy Scranton puts it in the title of his magnificent but dispiriting book about reckoning with the fatal consequences of this human-ravaged epoch.[8] Scranton uses his own experience as a U.S. Army soldier during the invasion of Iraq to center this notion of embracing the inevitability of death in order to marshal the will to continue living and fighting. That is the intellectual and moral challenge I want to take up in these chapters, and to invite you all to contemplate with me. How do we do this? And how especially do we do this in one of the densest crucibles of imperial, settler-colonial, racial, ecological, industrial trauma, that of the modern and contemporary U.S. South? How would an updated understanding of a Weird South, alive to the networks of damage but also of deliverance, move us from a politics of recognition to one of actual renovation?

You may sense in my language here the comparative nihilism of the other fields that I am invested in and which southern studies now converses with productively and provocatively: the nihilism of settler-colonial studies, of Indigenous studies, and of the stark new histories of racial capitalism. These fields are locked typically into an examination of the power dynamics by which some humans are more responsible than others for the crumbling ecosystems and the dehumanizing economies in which we live, and where some are victimized more than others by both the brutality of these systems and the havoc they have exacted upon our world.[9] As the dial spins ineluctably around the ineradicable center of Anthropocentrism even while the notion of a singular Anthropos becomes ever more illogical, ever more dramatically fractured by the conditions of capitalism and power, weirdness as a concept

6 *The Weird South*

attempts to break us out of these deadlocks. The question will be, of course, where instead the Weird South takes us, if not to another imaginative horizon or planet altogether.

Such escapes to "otherwise worlds" form the conceit for a recent collection of essays about contemporary Black and Indigenous speculative fictions asserting new possibilities and futures in the wake of devastating settler-colonial and racial capitalist histories.[10] Indeed, more and more scholars are taking up and taking *to* the deep time and occluded others embedded within the bedrock of Anthropocenic time and yet occluded as such. These subjectivities are in fact—as Kathryn Yusoff has argued—produced by the very "white Geology" that undergirds and typifies our ability to think its structures and forms. Yusoff draws on the instrumental work of black feminists such as Sylvia Wynter, Katherine McKittrick, Hortense Spillers, and Christina Sharpe, alongside other foundational thinkers in the arena of posthuman and new materialist thought, to cinch the materiality of blackness and of diaspora to violent imperial processes. Black and brown subjects are "ghosts," she contends, "of geology's epistemic and material modes of categorization and dispossession."[11] While acceding the political and historical specificities of differently racialized experiences, Yusoff nonetheless delineates a throughline of the sacrificial, absorbent, dark bodies—from sugarcane plantations to toxic reservations—that have always already predated the astonishment of the Anthropocene. In other words, as she puts it incisively, "the Anthropocene as a politically infused geology and scientific/popular discourse is just now noticing the extinction it has chosen to continually overlook in the making of its modernity and freedom."[12] The "proximity of black and brown bodies to harm," as central nodes in the conversion of geographical space to property and production and in the inhuman and dehumanizing processes of extraction, rises up urgently now for witness.[13] Yusoff's counterthrust is to posit these "billion" voided Black and Indigenous experiences of geopolitical formation predating scientists' fairly recent (circa 1950) recognition of an Anthropocenic

The Grave 7

age, an academic fiction that obscures the colonial-capitalist processes driven by these logics and dependent on their erasure.

Yusoff and others have thus begun to draw together the experience of differently racialized subjects into a conceptual continuity of kindred disruptions to the geopolitical dismissals of the Anthropocene. Elsewhere, I have targeted in particular the perceived exceptionalism of Indigenous culture, identity, and literary production within these discussions—in part because these presumptions serve an elite academic agenda more than, or at least as much as, they satisfy an important legal and political Indigenous will to separatism. To be sure, either because of or despite the politicized performance of ecological shamanism, Indigenous thinkers and artists are seen as the original posthumanists, preternaturally attuned to the weird ecological underpinnings that bedevil Anthropocenic hegemony. As such, many Indigenous philosophies and practices are now being regularly invoked as antidotes to climate disaster and routes toward alternative modes of sustainable habitation of our plant. So while "Weird Indigeneity" seems like a concept worthy of exploring, and I have certainly done so, it is largely in service of helping us to suss out the lie inherent to it: that the most fully weird and (to my mind) most energizing Indigenous thought is aware of itself as a byproduct of the very taxonomies from which we are trying to rescue ourselves, and resists the ideological off-ramps of exceptionalism in this regard, instead exercising (and thoroughly revising the concepts of) uncompromising complicity and inclusivity alike. This need not mean sacrificing Indigeneity in the process, as we might imagine or fear, but rather refashioning it as epiphanic, porous, and elemental. As Morton suggests, an "*indigeneity* to the symbiotic real" lingers as latent knowledge within humans generally and is therefore recoverable. By contrast, "the thing we keep telling ourselves with our words and our social space and our philosophy and our Stockholm syndrome feelings, that we are outside of [the geological and the natural and the consumer] world . . . is killing us and all life on this planet."[14]

Morton is almost certainly not talking about Indians per se but is invoking an idea(l) of "indigeneity" that has historically been both common and corrosive. And yet, if we can bracket for a moment the obvious proprietary conflict over Indigenous cultural knowledge engendered by his call,[15] it may offer us a charismatic tool for grasping the kinds of suppressed acquaintance with totality, with subscendence, and with interrelationality that preexist colonial, geographic, and agrilogistical rupture. In the final chapter, I reflect more directly on how "Indigenizing" the southern real can be both a red herring (pardon the pun) but can also potentially move us toward startling revelations about our shared collusion in so many of the systems we might think we can or should reject. But before we get there, we need to take up an initial grappling with the South as a cognate geography of meaning. Much like the multifaceted, global Indigenous experience, the South harbors a haunted legacy of brutal attempts to cleave the inhuman from the civilized, to disambiguate human from human, in ways that could never hold and which we need to acknowledge now in order to attempt to live in ways that are not escapist, fetishistic, or romantic. In doing so, I want to suggest that concepts like "Indigeneity" and "the South" in contemporary thought serve similarly as epistemes to either redeem or condemn, to rescue or to reprove. Rarely do we admit that such identities corral precisely what we fear: like any identity construct, and yet more palpably for their unique insularities, they are weird assemblages of all we have attempted to master, control, define, and repudiate.

Such an acknowledgement need not be destabilizing. Much like Yusoff and others, Morton encourages us to investigate the deep structures that give way to, and produce the inherent flaws in, Anthropocenic logic. But unlike other thinkers, Morton invites a ground-level view into the intimacy between human and inhuman others before and beyond the relations of power and the discriminatory logics that divide and sub-

The Grave 9

divide. Also unlike other posthumanist scholars, Morton's vantage is itself conceptually apocalyptic, destabilizing the very foundations of human correlationism (that is, the notion that things exist only insofar as we humans apprehend them). Other humans, other forms of life "do not simply live alongside us: they are within us. We are strangers to ourselves. That is how close the other is. Ecology is about intimacy."[16] Our very inability to be conscious of our devastating influence on the environment—which is also us, ourselves, our bodies—is a dismal predictor of our capacity to tune any sort of consciousness to the work of repair. The first order of business is thus embracing the tyranny by which the agrilogistical order, the lynchpin of the Anthropocene, insists on noncontradiction, tidiness, production—and interrogating the way that such logics conceal our weird, twisted coexistence with the unruly, the overgrown, the viral as well as the bounded, curtailed, and evacuated excess.

It should be apparent by now that the South's particular immiseration in agrologistic space and structuralism entails a unique estrangement and has produced vast legacies of violent ordering that implicated and disappeared Indigenous land rights and Black labor in turn. Neither the inheritance of such systematic interpellation, nor the ecological and human rights emergencies that outlive those processes, can be visible unless we surrender to the axiom of weird coexistence, to the terror of interpenetration and ambiguity. We live in—in fact, we *are*—the world that the slaves and the slaveholders made, to riff on Eugene Genovese's classic title. Ours is a biosphere that collapses worker, field, weevil, gin, noose—the myriad forms of exclusion, intrusion, and arrest that mark the South's passage from settler-colonial space to industrialized apartheid. This is an ontological enlargement that should come as an intrusive, existential shock, and one that forces the perversions of human-centered agency to redouble in visibility and consequence, because we see their effects so much more plainly and in their horrifyingly vast consequences. One benefit of this shattering-open is being able to—as Morton puts it—"un-

10   The Weird South

erase [nonhuman life forms] within Marxism,"[17] to access "a trapdoor in the ideological superstructure of capitalism,"[18] and thereby cease abstracting and abjecting the nonhuman from the human systems through the Anthropocenic mechanism by which all things are made real or not. Inversely, and most importantly, the dehumanized brown and Black bodies both integral to and evicted from these logics reappear in their material and materialized forms, spectral though they may now be.

This is a bleak, belated revelation that, at least at first, tends to frustrate rather than animate the reflexive responses of ethical repair and kinship that would be necessary to mend the rifts in all we have created and destroyed. Our tendency to sever human and material worlds from the nonhuman (broadly construed) is precisely what makes it possible for a "human" species to exist in any kind of solidarity. But when the criteria for personhood develop in a racialized, agrologistical regime, it threatens by default any hope of functional cohesion. That is to say, as much ardent critique has already affirmed, the "Anthropos" driving the Anthropocene cannot be attributed equally to all humans, and so our taxonomies of responsibility falter on the very same reductive, divisive logics that birth both racialized and Anthropocentric regimes. It is another kind of loop indeed, and perhaps weirdness is the way not to escape but to better understand the Möbius strip holding together everything that the Anthropocene has endeavored to blow apart. I want to remind us that our challenge is, must be, to arrive at some place of truly generative (re)action in response to all of this. But for this to be more than empty aspiration, we need to lay bare the ghosts beholding the trauma. Here I am distinguishing, as Avery Gordon does, between haunting and trauma: the former is the announcement of the latter, which sits in bodies and places, typically unwitnessed, unacknowledged. Haunting, Gordon tells us, heralds "that moment (of however long duration) when things are not in their assigned places, when the cracks and rigging are exposed, when the people who are meant to be

The Grave 11

invisible show up without any sign of leaving, when disturbed feelings cannot be put away, when something else, something different from before, seems like it must be done."[19]

Something *must be done*. Gordon's ghost hunt is interdisciplinary—she is a sociologist by training but is pointedly in search of knowledge that cannot be narrowly owned. In her quest, she privileges literary fiction for its imaginative license to manifest the unseen through its "ensemble of cultural imaginings, affective experiences, animated objects, narrative densities, and eccentric traces of power's presence."[20] Simply put, stories "open the door to understanding haunting," and such understanding is "essential for grasping the nature of our society and for changing it."[21] While Gordon's purview is largely sociological and historical, intent on exposing the horrors of racialized modernity, Morton's adds an explosive layer of phenomenological implication wherein ghosts are not aberrant but ordinary. In these freshly striated views of history and violence and ruptured privacy, the world we have made and our perceived place in it is, for good or ill, upended: "everything is uncanny, because we can't say for sure whether it's alive or not alive, sentient or not sentient, conscious or not conscious, and so on. Everything becomes spectral, undead, in all kinds of unique and different ways. So the struggle to have solidarity with lifeforms is the struggle to include specters and spectrality."[22] To graft onto Morton's pronouncement here the lexicon of southern studies: the struggle to inhabit the posthumanist biosphere is also the struggle to include, together, the miscellaneous, pusillanimous, threatful ghosts of settler colonialism, chattel slavery, and the various, vicious upendings that they continue to create and conceal.

So, to shift our view from the spectral to the material, from the ethereal to the earth, and from the ghost to the grave—that is, to see what is laid bare by our confrontations with the implosive real of the southern biosphere—I want to revisit some of the most well-traveled sites in southern Gothic terrain: the cemetery, the haunted house, the plantation. I am interested especially in scenes of burial and exhumation, like that in the Porter story with which I opened this chapter, as indices of what knowledge lies incipient but hidden, often forbidden, in the holes and caverns and structures we tend, till, tame, build, and inhabit, those testaments to the hubris and folly of imagining that we too might be impenetrable, protected, sovereign. Instead of telling the same awful ghost stories that inhere in haunted historical spaces, I want to appreciate instead how southern fiction has always labored to both expose and conceal the elemental truths of our landless, selfless, powerless condition. Once we consider speciesism and racism as part of the same delusional construct of separateness—the very misapprehension that renders exterminable those presumed to be not-like-us or less-than-human—then we can register, with appropriate horror, the correspondence between assaults like agricultural exhaustion, animal extinctions, chattel slavery, even genocide.

Here's what I am not doing: by treading into the historical epicenter of U.S. race relations and of racial capitalist perversities, as much new scholarship is currently doing, I am neither redressing the antagonisms or invoking alliances between Black and Indigenous subjects, entombed together but differentially at the conjoined sites of removal and dispossession. Nor am I parsing the (also differential) experiences of ownership and racialization based on land, labor, and body nor their ongoing impacts on both Indigenous and Black political and cultural formations. This is work being done with granular precision by scholars such as Alyosha Goldstein, Jodi Byrd, Shona Jackson, Iyko Day, Tiffany King, and Mark Rifkin, among others. While many of these interventions have productively disrupted the impasse between Afropessimist and Indigenous analytics, they have not necessarily liberated any particular subgroup from indenture within these codifying logics and histories. Nor can they. I am suggesting instead that we venture further into an imaginative exercise—not about where Indians and slaves and others are or are not in the archives, nor about where and how brown or Black or

The Grave 13

Indigenous praxis might overturn capitalist and colonialist systems, but rather about whether releasing ourselves entirely from the typical terms of engagement and affiliation might be the most emancipating move of all. In other words, if we conjure a different destination of aspiration, how might our route there change as a result? In 2005, Patricia Yaeger wrote an essay on "Ghosts and Shattered Bodies," which posed the question "*What Does It Mean to Still Be Haunted by Southern Literature?*" Nearly twenty years later, I am asking the same question, because neither Yaeger nor I intend to use the agony of aftermath to deny its aptness. *Of course* we are still haunted, and will perhaps always be haunted, but perhaps for reasons more terrifyingly complex and strange than we have yet acknowledged. Perhaps we are still haunted precisely because the ghosts are demanding a different ending, a new constellation of narratives that do justice to the fullness of their—of our shared—suffering. As theorist Donna Haraway puts it, we need in this moment "stories (and theories) that are just big enough to gather up the complexities and keep the edges open and greedy for surprising new and old connections" (160). New and old connections: that dialectic is the movement of these chapters.

Let's return briefly to Porter's story, which I offer as something of a template for this work. Set in 1903 and published in 1935, the story presents a bracing view into postplantation hauntedness that cracks open earth, graves, and bodies to uncover the tangled ecosystems within and among the boundaries we furiously tend. We learn immediately that the exhumed bones of Miranda's grandfather had already been "twice disturbed" by his wife—first in a move to Louisiana, and then to Texas, where they remained until the final relocation that forms the premise of the story (177). There are twenty other graves emptied here as well, mostly of Kentucky relatives who also migrated west, all of whom have been transferred to the "big new public cemetery." The reiterative removes—of an entire community or at least a family, it seems—are thus reflexive adaptations to the clan's diminishing claim on a past

14   *The Weird South*

of relative security: a chain of dispossessions met frankly by the "constancy and possessiveness" of the grandmother who clings to the remote vestiges of privacy and security, and whose land cannot be taken until after her death (177). But immediately Porter establishes an evocative motility along the fragile border between life and death, between states of rest and resurrection. She refers pointedly to the family "plot," not as simply a burial site but, importantly, a *narrative* of both origins and loss. Thus, in the geographical shift from slave South to progressive West, from private land to a public commons, she maps a story that is not proprietary and never could or should be. Instead, it is but one held in conjunction with that of so many others, in and especially beyond the plantation economy. It is this perceived reduction, and with it an utter destabilization of meaning and identity, that underscores much of the suppressed trauma of the story.

Appropriately, Miranda and Paul gaze at the rows of empty pits with a combination of "wonder" and "disappointment." The latter sentiment is prompted by the "commonplaceness of the actual spectacle," which is to say that the thrill of encountering the haunted holes is eclipsed by the tedium of absence: "when the coffin was gone," Miranda thinks, "a grave was just a hole in the ground" (178). The moment drives home the materiality of the scene, the fetish of preservation disambiguated from the raw reality of the earth's disclosures, and thus exposes the tyranny of a kind of epistemology whereby the spectral has no claim. Something must be seen to be experienced, and so far Miranda lives in a world overdetermined by appearances, one where she is shamed for dressing like a boy or riding bareback. The power of such corrections is the way that Miranda internalizes them so completely that she develops "a fine set of antennae radiating from every pore of her skin," an alert system that triggers deep shame as well as confusion when the social norms conflict with the religious "truths" repeated catechistically by her father. His dictates elevate "rigorous economy" over empty social graces, teaching her that "wastefulness was vulgar" and "a sin" (180).

The Grave 15

So much of the power of southern weirdness and spectrality is registered in and through the fine "antennae" of the body before the mind can organize its logic. Yet sometimes those circuits of transmission remain permanently disrupted by the myriad and contradictory signals the body receives. This is the quality that can lend the air of eeriness—pores electrified, a chill in the spine—signs that we often associate with the thrills of the Gothic. But in these texts they are indications of something more basely, expressly earthly: Weird texts register cues of dissonance, or wrongness, and dig deeper into the ground to circumvent the limits of our epistemological ignorance. Here, Miranda leaps literally from estrangement to affinity, jumping into her grandfather's grave and "scratching about aimlessly and pleasurably, as any young animal." She scoops and weighs the soil, which had a "pleasantly sweet, corrupt smell" (178). Overall, three variations of the word "pleasure" ("pleased"; "pleasurably"; and "pleasantly") appear in the space of about six sentences, a conspicuous redundancy for a writer whose style is painstakingly precise (177–78). Clearly, she wants to underscore the seductive affect, the raw experience of pleasure, here in this space that is other than human, and in doing so highlight how such experiences unleash the animal desire to root around sensuously in the vibrant matter that exists beyond and beneath human mortality and death's forms.

Disturbingly, this is also the unimaginable but now inhabitable space of social death, of removal, of estrangement from privilege and from the plantation South as a material reality. The ancestral bones traveling west mimic the pattern of Indigenous removal (in particular, the Choctaws' diligence of carrying ancestral bones along their migration route), a rhetorical move typical of modern southern anxieties about nativism and dispossession.[23] The extirpations are conveyed as blunt, cavernous, residual, intergenerational, and ongoing. But the weird thrill of loss is an ecstatic punctuation—in the bare sense of the word "ecstasy," meaning to stand apart from the self[24]—as the story returns over and over again to a world

16 *The Weird South*

demarcated by a corrosive materialism that supersedes, in fact buries, these existential expeditions. What the children find left behind by the coffins, then, is more immediately legible than the sublime pleasures of the earth's openings themselves, or the trinkets they discover within them: Miranda finds a small silver dove, which is actually the screw head for a coffin, and Paul retrieves a "wide gold ring carved with intricate flowers and leaves" (178). It is no accident that both objects are replicas of natural elements—animal and vegetable—rendered in precious metals, nonhuman passengers subsumed within an economy that assigns value only in forms fungible for human custody.

What happens next underscores the fatal grip of such logics in the postplantation southern economy, particularly for those peripheral southerners who exist on the margins of its toppled hierarchies. In this case, these marginal figures no longer (or in Porter's own case, never) gain elite purchase simply via the privilege of whiteness. The family's economic and social precarity suffuses the story, is in fact the framing anxiety precipitating its events, and the children register it. Thus, while the found objects represent outsized value to the children, prompting great excitement and a feverish trade, they also elicit shame. After receiving the ring from Paul, Miranda puts it on her finger and immediately says, "Maybe we ought to go now . . . maybe one of the niggers'll see us and tell somebody." Feeling "like trespassers," they flee a scene where their bereftness might be exposed by the leveling gaze of African American others who would by default expose their fraud and perhaps also their theft (178). This escape briefly protects them and safeguards their treasures, and it sets up the story's second half. A hunting "expedition," which is by all measures an affirmation of southern white male hegemony, is made somewhat hysterical by a combination of youthful ignorance and acculturated anxiety.

The story's climactic event serves as a revelation of the complex suppressions levied against women in particular. Both children are hunting, but while Paul shoots to kill, Mi-

The Grave 17

randa simply likes "pulling the trigger and hearing the noise." Further, she "always followed at Paul's heels . . . obeying instructions" and "learning" (179). The densities of Miranda's subjugation are redoubled by the ring, whose glittery novelty distracts her entirely, and prompts in her a desire to go home and clean her "grubby" body and sit idle in fancy clothes. "These things were not all she wanted, of course," the narrator tells us, but they are the most immediately available signifiers of wealth to accompany her new accessory. They satisfy in the moment the "vague stirrings of desire for luxury and a grand way of living which could not take precise form in her imagination, being founded on a family legend of past wealth and leisure" (180). Again, desire and pleasure and "legend" trump reality, which is grubby, oppressive, violent. While she lags behind in the comfort of her fantasy, Paul coolly shoots a rabbit—"right through the head," he reports. Miranda watches as Paul expertly skins and opens the animal's body, revealing an "oddly bloated belly." The rabbit was pregnant (181).

What is "odd" about this supremely natural maternal state, one which can't be an unusual sight for these children accustomed to the wilderness, yet nonetheless arrests both in amazement? On the one hand, it functions as a signifier of the gulf between the natural and the social real, a squelching of Miranda's young animal pleasures in favor of obedience, denial, propriety. At the same time, Porter wants us to see the oddness of this oddity—its weirdness, if you will. An uncanny interruption, presaged by the brief view into the empty graves, exposes the elemental cords connecting the unquiet earth, the slaughtered rabbit and babies, and these precarious children, arrested between youth and maturity, possession and dispossession, luxury and poverty, knowledge and ignorance. The natural world functions again as a template, a lesson laid bare, about the tangled operations of pleasure and grief, desire and subjugation, of killing as authority and increase, and of the terrible consequences of human dominion. It is no mistake that Paul shifts to "Brother" in this moment, and eventually to "the brother," an expansive allegory and a

18 *The Weird South*

drifting detachment for the masculine pedagogy Miranda is about to suffer.

As this brother—any brother—dissects the rabbit further and exposes the tiny, aborted rabbits in their mother's womb, Miranda is mesmerized and tutored: "Oh, I want to *see*," she says, "under her breath"—a desire she can't quite utter aloud. She watches, rapt, "excited but not frightened, for she was accustomed to the sight of animals killed in hunting—filled with pity and astonishment and a kind of shocked delight in the wonderful little creatures for their own sakes, they were so pretty" (182). Animal deaths are ordinary and marginal, their lives presenting to the children as "disorderly and unaccountably rude . . . but altogether natural and not very interesting." But this particular scene quickly becomes intimate. The "wonderful little creatures" strike Miranda as lovely, and when she touches one of them "ever so carefully," noticing "'there's blood running over them,'" she "began to tremble without knowing why." The connection is physical and electric, and it awakens in her an immediate knowledge which "having seen, she felt at once as if she had known all along. The very memory of her former ignorance faded, she had always known just this" (182). This is not an epiphany per se, although it resembles one. Rather, the realization Miranda comes to is always already encoded in her body, registered by her antennae, but its implications are not straightforward or even legible. What is most important here is the brief independence of access. She has always relied on others for information or direction, and of course "no one had ever told her anything outright." Opportunities to learn about the elemental facts of life, as it were, abounded in her view but "she had been rather unobservant of the animal life around her because she was so accustomed to animals," and also effectively blind to their "rude" and "disorderly" irrelevance. As the younger, female sibling, she knows that ignorance is her lot, yet Porter indicates the fragility and performativity of that assumption: "Her brother had spoken as if he had known about everything all along. He may have

The Grave 19

seen all this before. He had never said a word to her, but she knew now a part at least of what he knew" (182).

Miranda's inheritance of this knowledge is abrupt and enlivening, but it is also punitive. Rather than liberating her, the "secret, formless intuitions in her own mind and body" become warnings "which had been clearing up, taking form, so gradually and so steadily she had not realized she was learning what she *had to know*" (182, emphasis added). She realizes that the young rabbits had been killed just before they could be born, "like kittens . . . like babies," and she becomes "terribly agitated" (182). Paul realizes that this knowledge, once "forbidden," has edged closer to Miranda's human consciousness, and he becomes anxious to suppress it once again: "Paul buried the young rabbits again in their mother's body, wrapped the skin around her, carried her to a clump of sage bushes, and hid her away . . . 'Listen now,' he tells Miranda, 'Now you listen to me, and don't ever forget. Don't you ever tell a living soul that you saw this. Don't tell a soul . . . Now, that's a secret. Don't you tell'" (183). Paul's motive is self-protection—he doesn't want their father to know he had led her "into things you ought not to do"—but Miranda's own impulse is similarly evasive. She "never told" and "did not even wish to tell anybody" (183).

Miranda doesn't tell, but Porter does. She unveils a world and a moment where the most elemental self-knowledge and truths are forcibly blocked or buried in an effort to maintain (or to manufacture) coherence amid the chaos of cultural evolution and the uprooting from land, legacy, and automatic privilege. Those principles remain urgent in this scene, to be sure, but they are interrupted by Miranda's brusque realization of her own detention and implication within their largely patriarchal logics. This awareness first arouses and then petrifies her, quite literally, into silence. The secrets she voluntarily keeps both define and destroy her; the knowledge is integral and intimidating all at once. But what is it, exactly? What does Miranda learn? Many scholars have been satisfied with a surface reading that suggests, as James William Johnson puts it, "obviously, and simply, [this is] the story of a young girl's first realization of the nature of love and sex."[25] Perhaps "obvious," but far from simple (except maybe to a male literary scholar writing in 1960), this knowledge both exposes and exceeds the ordinary gambit of a woman's sober coming-of-age and instead orbits the entirety of U.S. southern historical trauma. It is against this backdrop that readers encounter Miranda entombed primally in haunted space yet keening toward a shattering vista of shared biological vulnerability, of radical connection that disturbs forever all sense of exceptional human preeminence, and with it the overlay of power differentials fixed in race, class, and geographic ideologies and identities. This is why the emptied graves and the emptied womb abut experientially in this spare narrative, giving up horrifying discoveries that must be stolen, hidden, buried, and denied.

The idea of the traditional southern Gothic has already been revised by an expanse of new scholarship that urges attention less to the spectacular than to the ordinary. The "excess, monstrosity, perversion, nightmares, [and] rattling machinery," as Yaeger puts it, "give way to less operatic forms," ones where "fragments, residues, or traces of trauma fashion a regime of haunting . . . odds and ends that denote the unseen."[26] In her taxonomy, the "remnant" functions as an especially powerful reminder of what has been lost or torn away, revealing in the process "part-bodies that are not psychic delusions but physical facts." These remnants function as stand-ins for a whole, constitutive system ruined by its internal excisions and by the dispensable others whose gutting lingers and haunts. They work to supply "add-on[s] that [are] at once necessary and missing, an increment that gestures toward a person, a community, or world-that-would be."[27] Similarly, in a much more capacious context, Morton describes the apprehension of weird relationality as a holism with "a piece missing. Something doesn't add up, in a disturbing way,"[28] because the politics of coexistence are "always contingent, brittle, and flawed."[29]

Much of Morton's and Yaeger's language here in fact

The Grave 21

echoes that of Porter's story, as she works to signify the shock of recognition that her young female character experiences in witnessing a slain, eviscerated body at once unaccountably alien and chillingly familiar. The rabbit's violated, expunged part-body and its aborted babies arrest Miranda into tacit confrontation with her own motherless, adjunctive status: a girl struggling to meet the expectations of a world of fathers and brothers and ungenerous voyeurs. (We know from Porter's own biography that her mother died in childbirth with another sibling when Porter was just a toddler, making this incident even more resonant.) Race is almost entirely absent from the scene, at least in any explicit sense, partly because the children have so anxiously fled its surveillance. But this is where Porter's sublimation works to disarm us. Miranda's indoctrination is into a world free from the ignorance of election, which is to say that the disorderly, rude, yet intimate presence of animals in her orbit becomes manifest as an unthought, unarticulated known: a truth never told outright and yet internalized deeply. Certain lesser-than-human creatures are vulnerable to violence both mercenary and recreational, and none of it and none of them matter in the above-ground, stitched-up, covered-over world.

Yaeger focuses, as does so much southern literary production, on the perspective of the child who, like Miranda, seems to have privileged access to these scraps of knowledge and eruptions of "the unthought known"—Yaeger's phrase for "the omnipresence of ideas in southern literature that are *known* but not *acknowledged*," emerging fitfully in fragments, traces, grams, assemblages in an atmosphere of uncanny.[30] In contemporary speculative and posthuman contexts, the child is often figured as a portal or vehicle to the utopian imaginary, somewhat akin to the Indigenous trope: as gateways to presocial innocence, or to a magical state of animistic, premodern unity that might rescue us from "the modern idea of human exceptionalism [that] has alienated and disenchanted the world," as Benjamin Boysen puts it.[31] The southern version of this trope tends to frustrate such deliverance, slipping disturbingly from such revelations to the trauma of their witness. Of Porter's fictional landscape generally, Yaeger observes, there is "the burning sense that all around us, and all around the child, there is an excess or remainder. Something is calling out from Miranda's past that escapes the control of its concepts, that continues to weep." "[T]he child," she continues, "becomes the agonized vehicle for this lost remainder."[32]

Most disturbing in "The Grave" is the idea that what Miranda learns—the "unthought known" that she finds now she "had to" confront—is couched in the intimacy of the natural, yet teaches in fact an imperial, dominating ethos that the men and boys in her world already apparently know. It is a lesson about the potential of her own body to be ripped open and apart, curtailed and controlled, stitched together and suppressed. Of course, it is most chillingly a threatful warning about the biological consequences of desire, the animal pleasure she touches in the exposed grave juxtaposed against the sterile institutional promise of the gold ring and the comparative safety it harbors. The final message, then, is about sheathing that desire, looking askance at the consequences it may produce, and a crushing, obliterating disregard for the legion others—animal, dark, female—subordinated to patriarchal authority.

But desire and secrets linger, and they haunt. Because he is not female, Paul is able, almost hypnotically, to command Miranda to quell both. Not only does she never tell, but she doesn't even "wish" to—a fitting conclusion to a story already marked by covertness and white anxiety about the incriminating gaze of subjected others. Miranda is briefly disturbed by the entire incident—not just the slain rabbit and babies, apparently, but everything that transpires in the frame of the story's telling—and she does think about the "*whole* worrisome affair with confused unhappiness for a few days," until it "sank quietly into her mind and was heaped over by accumulated thousands of impressions, for nearly twenty years" (183, emphasis added). The locution here is not subtle: in a

The Grave 23

story about gravedigging and womb excavating, we know that the "heaped over" mind will eventually be unpacked and exposed. This happens nearly two decades later while Miranda is in Mexico, where Porter herself lived and worked during the 1920s supporting and documenting the revolution and identifying passionately with the peasants, the workers, and the Indigenous fighting desperately for better lives. We also know that Porter became pregnant and had an abortion while there, sometime in the early 1920s.[33] Porter places Miranda in the same place at about the same time—around 1923 (180).[34] These biographical details underscore the traumatic resurgence "from its burial place before her mind's eye" while "picking her path among the puddles and crushed refuse of a market street in a strange city of a strange country" (183). As a trigger for the uncanny, Porter again uses a "strange" scene; the descriptor is in fact repeated twice in close succession to underscore the alienness—another way of suggesting that the weird is a constant passenger embedded in the body's knowing but also forbidden to surface except by summons, given the right conditions. Porter's grammar here confirms the lie: the memory was never gone but uneasily interred "*before* her mind's eye," an adjusted colloquialism (from the more common "*in* one's mind's eye,"[35] which would imply a more internalized imagining), suggesting that it is both in and out of view at the same time. In other words, the memory is "hidden in plain sight," to use John T. Matthews's phrase for the phenomenon by which slave capitalist realities are occluded in order for the illusion of white supremacy and moral rectitude to persist.[36]

Here is where the weirdness of Porter's vision erupts, via Miranda's sublimated view into that epiphanic childhood day, which was never simply about the family graves, the treasures, or the slaughtered rabbit family. Importantly, it is the palimpsest of a market scene that forces the unthought known to suddenly clarify: "in totality, plain and clear in its true colors" (183). It is a hot day, amplifying the discordant smells of "raw flesh and wilting flowers," bringing her back in

Proustian fashion to "the mingled sweetness and corruption she had smelled that other day in the empty cemetery at home: the day she had remembered vaguely always until now as the time she and her brother had found treasure in the opened graves." The jarring return of the memory also alters what "until now" had been something innocuous, even pleasant, a selective favoring of "treasure" over trauma. But here, she knows without saying—and even without knowing, exactly— that the day signified something far darker. She is, abruptly, "so *reasonlessly* horrified she halted suddenly staring, the scene before her eyes dimmed by the vision back of them" (183, emphasis added). What is she seeing that prompts this irrational, visceral horror?: "An Indian vendor had held up before her a tray of dyed-sugar sweets, shaped like all kinds of small creatures: birds, baby chicks, baby rabbits, lambs, baby pigs. They were in gay colors and smelled of vanilla, maybe . . . (183). Pointedly, it is an "Indian vendor" who prompts Miranda's double vision, holding up the tray of candy animals as a kind of lens to an unredemptive past, to a phenomenology that disturbs without salvation. It is not even irony but something more insidious that positions the Indian as the merchant to the exchange, peddling instead of animism a commodified substitution that collapses the mystified distinctions between animal, human, nature, object, and merchandise—all inextricable and mutually produced and packaged. And yet, even while implicated, the Indian guide briefly prompts a more primordial consciousness normally occluded by the torsions of modernity. As I suggested, we will see more fully in the final chapter that such Indigenous apertures are little more than heterotopias, part of the assemblage of wishful idealisms and compensatory pleasures ushered forth by Anthropocenic despair.

Lying beneath the memory of treasure in the open graves are the baby rabbits from the mother's grave-womb that, once closed over on itself and hidden away, disappeared from her consciousness. Yet this imperfectly repressed knowledge does haunt Miranda's adulthood the way it had always already

The Grave 25

typified her childhood without her consent. Like Faulkner's Isaac (Ike) McCaslin (the young narrator who in *Go Down Moses* discovers the plantation ledgers that divulge horrifying secrets about his family's brutal entanglement in the lives and bodies of their chattel), we get the sense that Miranda is similarly haunted by her brief glimpse into the tangled cords of postplantation, patriarchal cruelty. Upon their disturbing correction of his genealogical record, Faulkner's Ike quickly internalizes the accounts' impact: "he would never need to look at the ledgers again" in order to register their permanent influence on his own life and psyche, "nor did he" (57). Miranda, too, needn't look directly but only askance, suppressing in her "mind's eye" the knowledge that she can't bear to witness straight on. Its abidance is filtered through the triggering shapes and smells of a meat market, where "piles of raw flesh" and the saccharine replicas of baby animals are rendered as consumable confections, the harsh reality and the palatable commodity suspended in terrible juxtaposition. Like Ike, Miranda doesn't need to literally see the mobile, haunting facts and figures of a brutal and expansive economy of corruption to understand her own implication in it, to corrode the sweetness of her exile, to "know" what she never knew she knew—what she was perhaps trying not to know. As Sarah Robertson has shown, reading the full cycle of Miranda stories published in *The Old Order*, silence and reticence are key conditions for the family to maintain its sense of moral coherence in the face on its past and ongoing entanglement in Black labor. Throughout, a young Miranda, in those intervening years between the day of treasure and the horror of its return, "begins the process of piecing together a hidden family history: she is involved in filling in what Malcolm Bull terms 'the void left by the hiddenness of truth'" (9). The Gay family's narrative is one marred by gaps: omissions that pivot around the interconnectedness between miscegenation, black labor, and blood-knowledge"[37]—not unlike the secrets interred within Faulkner's fatal dynasties.

Biographer and critic Mary Titus demonstrates the elemental gap at the epicenter of Miranda's—and Porter's—reconstruction of the past and her family history, namely the death of her mother two months after childbirth and the permanent association between fertility and death that would haunt her thereafter. What the other stories in *The Old Order* amplify vividly is the ideal of the grandmother, who bore eleven children and tended lovingly, along with her Black domestic servants, to their offspring as well as the many fruit trees and the landscapes surrounding her country and town homes. This vision of fecundity and, indeed, "order" starkly contrasts the actual, rude poverty of Miranda's upbringing and the guttering loss at its origin. The mingled sweetness and corruption of "The Grave" makes devastating sense when we consider its yoking together of "sexual terror" and romantic nostalgia for a redeemed and repopulated past—replete with the people, including slaves—that flesh out, quite literally, her homeless, motherless, landless existence.[38] "The Grave" ends, not surprisingly then, with poignancy following horror. Just as "instantly" as it had returned to her, "the dreadful vision faded, and she saw clearly her brother, whose childhood face she had forgotten, standing again in the blazing sunshine, again twelve years old, a pleased sober smile in his eyes, turning the silver dove over and over in his hands" (183).

Porter leaves us here with the structures of refusal and surrender that we see repeated throughout the twentieth century and beyond, from authors situated variously in relationship to the indelible residues of U.S. southern histories and logics but almost always somewhere on its occluded edge or periphery, where such sidelong exposures are both inevitable and necessary. First is the compulsive return, again and again, to sources of pleasure (Paul's "pleased" smile and the overall nostalgia of the remembered scene) rather than the more dreadful aspects that shadow them. The process is "instant" and apparently as effortless as the initial surrender of the knowledge gained that day to the quieted depths of Miranda's being. What loosens the lock on the more ghastly image,

The Grave 27

if only briefly, appears to be its strange, transnational setting with, if you will, its weird and expansive capacity to call up a suppressed memory of domestic terror. Here, Paul's youthful innocence and the collective incorruptibility of their childhood returns as a wishful mirage. And here, I would argue, is where the weirdness of weird southern texts becomes distinctly uneasy. On the one hand, it can offer arresting portals into the disruptive, leveling significance of our relationship to nonhuman things (broadly construed)—objects, animals, other life forms, natural elements—and thus into the precarity of normative, exclusionary hierarchies and their violences. On the other hand, inevitably, these discoveries instigate competing revelations, ones where the artifacts of modernity and especially capitalist production exist alongside their "natural" progenitors, and where neither the metallic nor the saccharine substitutes nor the raw, fleshly evocations of the uncanny has special claim. Miranda's double vision is exactly that: a function of a modern propulsion to know and see what is advantageous, not necessarily what is true, but never to jettison the partial knowledge that underlies and undermines the coherence of ethical identity and the indissoluble bonds between victim and victimizer.

In the end, Porter concludes—as we might, too, but not quite yet—that we have no real choice but to return to the worlds we have made, to the Anthropocentric narratives that seal the gaps and the bodies. To root around like an animal in a hole, as Miranda briefly does, is to render the grave a semiotic interpretation of what is otherwise just a hole in the ground, momentarily teeming with abundance rather than negation, with squirming living presence rather than extradited ghosts. But it turns out to be no place to live without abandoning a self whose coordinates—albeit self-denying—exist in the structures of the aboveground world, one of forgetting, and of pleasure palaces rather than sepulchers of loss. Titus links tightly to "The Grave" another story in *The Old Order*, "The Fig Tree," which features a younger Miranda who ritualistically buries dead animals and decorates their graves, and

28   *The Weird South*

who once suffers the fear that she has buried a chicken alive and can hear it crying: "From the earth beneath her feet came a terrible, faint troubled sound. 'Weep weep, weep weep . . .' murmured a little crying voice from the smothering earth, the grave." Eventually, her great aunt explains that the sound is actually that of the tree frogs, and Miranda relaxes: "They were in the trees," not buried alive in the earth.[39]

Miranda's marginal status as a poor white woman gives her tantalizing purchase into the abandonment of weird desire, vacillating between the open grave and the closed womb. But it also fixes her permanently into the dark matter of the web, which necessarily includes all we have rendered, extracted, perverted, split, and shaped—and so, weird eruptions haunt such characters in those interstices between. In the chapters that follow, I explore what happens to these graves—the holes, the wombs, the wounds, and the tombs of the mind— where humanity goes to die and be reborn; where the secrets of the South sustain themselves; and where its inheritors can find pleasure, nostalgia, even love in the faces of their destroyers, their victims, and their kin all at once, the way Miranda treasures Paul's "pleased sober smile" as he "turns the dove over and over in his hands." Porter invites us to witness along with Miranda the seduction of the spectacle, the sweetness of corruption, the hands that caress and kill, that smooth and silence—the very same hands. It amounts to a sleight of hand, in the end, that produces the unthought known out of thin air, and then makes it disappear again as if it never existed.

We will look especially in the next two chapters at the organicism and the peril of this phenomenon for those southerners aligned most fatally with the disposable ecologies in which they are embedded; where the natural and the built worlds share tortured space; where land, trees, forest become crop, house, civilization; and where human bodies are not gods wielding machines but are corroded parts, branches, cogs, and levers. The weirdness of the Weird South for these southerners especially is less the mannered, willed double vision of Porter and more the catastrophe of obliteration followed by

The Grave 29

a kind of graceful turn toward newness. These openings lie in the moments of witness and resurgence, sometimes emancipatory but often overwhelmingly bleak, and they entreat us to look beyond the human-centered fictions of power that we thought were the bottom of the well of trauma. Through the looking glass of posthumanism and all the postlandscapes of contemporary thought are more destabilizing archives still. The question is whether or not we can live there, or whether the same hands that have shaped, determined, produced, and violated us will ever consent to let us go.

CHAPTER 2

The Trees

The last chapter ended on a despondent note: the recognition that weird reality makes itself known in flashes of insight and connections that surface briefly only to return deep underground, packed away into settler-colonial and plantation cemeteries, into mind-graves and subliminal, subterranean spaces so that the theater of social, cultural, and racial normativity can persist aboveground. And yet these underground revelations simmer and disturb. What is epiphanic about weird *southern* writing is the way the earth's disclosures erupt and disrupt, not simply with the usual tools of post-traumatic shock or spectacular hauntings, but with more quiet, arresting confrontations with the unthought known; with the truths of human fragility laid bare; and especially with penetrations of the earthly and the natural landscapes and wombs that reveal their uncanny, refractive interiors. What functions as true horror in a story like "The Grave" is the recognition that the catechistic "truths" circulating above the earth's crust, the commandments and the imperatives, have the power to close the slain and exposed bodies, to stitch together violated wombs, to bury again the other-than-human victims in shallow graves where the earth will conceal and consume them in perverse kinship, never to be seen again—except sidelong, or in the blurred dual vision

31

of willed overlooking, buried in plain sight, weeping in the earth and the trees.

In this chapter, then, I want to explore the process of decomposition. That is, what happens when the raw materials that compose our social lives—the earth, the trees, the organisms, the mechanisms—collapse into the structures and the bodies we inhabit, that assemble the hiding places for the vast networks and the terrible secrets and trades that keep our networked selves alive? Weird southern texts entreat us to turn the architecture of this world inside out, to see the trees—literal and metaphorical—that become the planks of our existence, of our houses, and of our bodies, planks that eventually form the coffins for our secrets.

In her pivotal book on haunting, Avery Gordon borrows Toni Morrison's concept of "furniture without memories" to describe the way our built environment is laden with histories of violence and power and how that environment supports and shores us up without disclosing the matter of its making or its manipulations by prior occupants. She explains such furnishings as "power structures whose existence we navigate daily without questioning it. The chair we sit in, that shapes our posture, whose structure guides what we see and how comfortable we feel"—the depressions in the couch cushions that we sink into, where presence is legible only as after-the-fact absence.[1] Where Morrison uses the metaphor tangibly in her fiction, Gordon applies it more broadly to indicate the ways our modern ecosystems are replete with forms both material and subliminal that strangle into silence the signs of human dominion, both announcing and concealing the violence of their production.

So much of the literature from the postplantation South, where coerced and inequitable labor has shaped and surrendered so extensively, is haunted by ponderous questions: Can the negative shape speak? Can the losses ever be reconstituted? Can the memories and the extractions be restored to the material remainders that testify to sacrifice, or is the sublimation and the decomposition complete? Are the experiences

32 *The Weird South*

of double vision, the spectral spine-tingling, the sinking depression all inevitable legacies of brutal social systems whose operations are closed, complete, discrete? Can the body be more than a womb-grave for the removals and secrets and silences that suture it closed? Can furniture ever remember its trees?

Of course, I am not talking only (or even really) about trees, but about trees as a metonym for the elemental material of an agrilogistical economy. The concrete features of a local plantationscape have been converted into the means of accumulative wealth for a landowning white master class and into the identities, bodies, and suffering of African labor that was instrumental in shepherding forth the forms of this prosperity. These same features are evacuated of their own integrity in the process. I am focusing here on plantation and postplantation architectures and their creators in order to explore the potential for disambiguation in spaces where white precarity and coerced Black labor dissolve conjointly into the equipment of a social order that requires both to exist. This is, I would suggest, what Porter opens the door to witness when she shifts the weeping of the possibly alive chicken underground to the frogs in the yard: she embraces the weird essentialism by which the buried-alive weeping and the voices in the trees might in fact be one and the same, an echoic affirmation of Morton's ecognosis. And yet, Miranda cannot shake a correlationist view of reality, whereby things are real only if they are seen and acknowledged; hers is a strategy that supports not just empirical reality but its ideological mystifications. Put simply, it serves Great Aunt Eliza and in turn Miranda to hear the earth's mournful weeping as frogs' full-throated croaking in the trees rather than as a chicken slowly suffocating below ground. The stakes in my reading are thus at first illustrative: they make visible that which is obscured in a granular way that, apropos of new materialism, conjures the elemental aspects, the "thingness" of postplantation haunting, to be unraveled from the obliterating gaze, hands, and suppressions of white mastery and hegemony. Read in the way I propose

The Trees 33

here, these elemental aspects—animals, trees, and Black bodies—share an ecstatic space of loss and, from there, perhaps, provide an entry into weird reintegration and regenerativity.

To do so, I must first echo African American poet Tiana Clark's title to her arresting collection: *I Can't Talk about the Trees without the Blood*. For Clark and for us, the trees from which innumerable Black bodies were hung, tortured, lynched can never again be innocent symbols of a pastoral landscape. We live instead in the shattering aftershocks of racial capitalism's twisted logics and controls, saturating an environment where trees are indelibly marked by their implication and where furniture is always stained invisibly by the blood of its perverse construction. Poetry like Clark's makes the trees speak, blood and all, and so does some of the most unnerving and surgical new work emerging from Black American literature more broadly, which resists the silence of annihilation—the mood of much anti-Black, Afropessimist critique.[2] As Clark puts it in a 2021 poem,

> Black bodies are buried in the stickiness of history
> every day bodies become the next viral death. And yet, each day
> I want to write a poem about pleasure. Black pleasure.[3]

Pleasure from and in the midst of death? But how? Clark confronts the "stickiness" of history for the Black body, buried alive in so many layers of loss and death, and forges ahead with the pursuit of joy. The weird realities of our twisted, sticky entanglements don't allow for disambiguation necessarily, but perhaps for punctuations of relief through the recognition of aliveness and the possibilities of pleasure in the weave. But in attending to these new posthuman forays of African American experience here, and to Indigenous experience in the final chapter, we risk repeating what has been distinctly regressive about the ontological turn. Indeed, by claiming radical personhood for individuals whose affinity to animal and plant life has been a strategy for their subjugation, prominent in Enlightenment discourse and colonial administrations, posthumanist thought risks deepening rather than

34 *The Weird South*

relieving the collective debasement of nonhuman, parahuman, and subjugated individuals. Particularly in the plantation complex, "the conjunction of the colonial natural world and colonized human beings" was so complete that slaves were rendered features and functionaries of an ecosystem in need of taming.[4] Recognizing this imbrication need not perpetuate this haunting legacy but might instead invite us, in Monique Allewaert's view, to appreciate slaves' powerful role within an assemblage of agencies nourishing subaltern individuals throughout the colonies—an ecosystem where Black subjects harnessed the healing powers of the natural world in quiet acts of sustenance and creation.[5] Likewise, a new study by Zakiyyah Iman Jackson looks at an abundance of twentieth-century African diasporic literary and visual productions that "creatively disrupt the human-animal distinction and its persistent raciality," moving us potently beyond "a critique of bestialization to generate new possibilities for rethinking ontology."[6]

Allewaert and Jackson are at the vanguard of a pivot in the Afropessimist and Black feminist traditions, along with scholars like Joshua Bennett, Alexander Weheliye, Calvin Warren, Kevin Quashie, Christina Sharpe, Jennifer Nash, and others. Such work counters what has been morally stymieing in the new materialisms, which do little to relieve the stark disparities of human collusion and therefore accountability required in this particular moment. Instead, they redress the vast settler-colonial, racial capitalist, and starkly ecological and humanitarian devastation inflicted by centuries of unchecked Anthropocenic despotism that requires not just reflexive action but also ethical interrogation into the architecture of collapse. A closer look at weird southern texts that chronicle the passage from slavery's radical decompositions into these expanding webs of agency and identity might prompt such generative conceptions of a universe keening for reintegration. But the first step is to disaggregate the parts. It is time to untangle the trees from the forest, from the furniture, from the bodies that absorbed and erased them, in order to articulate

The Trees 35

the histories that rendered them inextricable parts of an unsettled, "sticky" whole. So, in this chapter, I want to suggest ways that weird southern imaginings might conjure forth a new, unruly, procreant materialism of the once and forever enslaved body out of the radical *dis*organization—the propulsive fracturing of bodies within an annihilating economic, social, and ideological system.

Let's begin, as we did in the last chapter, in a slightly earlier literary moment by navigating the traumatic transition between a determining plantation past and a new social order and space still fettered to the racialized logics of bound labor and white privilege, and indelibly haunted by its totalizing, eviscerating productions. We saw Porter's white narrator become acutely aware of the way Black and white perspectives converge to demystify the frail pretensions of power, and thus how this intertwining reflexively retreats from the threat of the Black gaze as well as the instigating presence of the Indigenous. Likewise, African American texts similarly acknowledge the Möbius-like interracial loops by which the Plantationocene's social fabric is rendered: a complete product in which the brutally elemental parts no longer have integrity. Let's start with a profoundly disturbing expression of this "strange couple"—the bundled unit of the white master and the Black female slave—in Charles Chesnutt's extraordinary short story "The Dumb Witness," written in 1897 and collected in his *The Conjure Woman and Other Conjure Tales*.[7]

Chesnutt's title announces immediately that this tale of "witness" will not be direct, or even necessarily audible, but will therefore in some way dramatize the multiply compressed layers of silence and violence that typify the afterlives of slavery. Chesnutt is frequently acknowledged as the first Black novelist, although he was so light skinned that he was capable of passing as white (this "option" is the haunting premise of much of his most famous work, including *The House Behind the Cedars* [1900]). Exploring both the ruse and reality of color as a hypervisible signifier of an often utterly immaterial condition was Chesnutt's passion, fueling his work as

36 *The Weird South*

not just a writer but also an educator and political activist for Black civil rights in the early twentieth century; he served on the newly formed NAACP and worked alongside W. E. B. Du Bois and Booker T. Washington, among other influential Black leaders of the time. From this authorial perspective, we enter the first-person narration of a white wealthy landowner: a northern carpetbagger and speculator who enters the scene from the margins of region and culture, and bears witness to the weird—in fact deeply disturbing—entanglements of the old world and the new. The story is told to him by the Black servant who works for him.

Through these manifold lenses and under the auspices of a potential timber purchase, we along with the white narrator come upon "the old Murchison place"—a once-grand plantation now in disrepair. We can hear the word "merchant" subsumed in the estate's name, an immediate signifier of the mercenary relationships underlying place, context, and identity, both historical and extant, in these overlaid postplantation scenes. Chesnutt's narrator is painstaking in his description of the decayed grandeur of the setting, the once-elegant and massive ornamental gateposts at the entrance to the estate now overgrown with "rank weeds and grass." Everything about the scene is contorted by the resurgence of vegetable and animal life, with a rattlesnake winding insidiously through the weeds, and even a "massive hinge" hanging loose and rust-eaten, "wrought" by time and the elements "into a fantastic shape" (158). The big house itself is "partly concealed," its former dominance amid the "well ordered pleasaunce" now obscured by the "wild and tangled profusion" of "trees and shrubbery" so enmeshed that "it was difficult to distinguish one bush or tree from another" (159). There is something distinctly eerie in the description of the scene, which arrests the viewer at once with the overwhelming abundance of natural forces encroaching on a structure where human agency and mastery have been distinctly deposed, the house seemingly "untenanted" and haunted by fantastic shapes of loss. But quickly, as the watcher draws nearer to the visage, the lens

The Trees 37

clarifies, and "the house stood clearly revealed" in its enduring if blighted magnificence.

Immediately visible in the proscenium are two figures on the house's long front piazza: at one end, an old white man seated in a "massive arm chair of carved oak," and at the other, an old woman "looking toward her vis-à-vis"—that is, "face to face," used in its archaic noun form to underscore their mirroring likeness, and in the possessive to bind the figures together more intimately. Indeed, although seemingly differently raced, the woman is obviously related "in some degree, unless this inference was negatived by the woman's complexion, which disclosed a strong infusion of darker blood" (159–60). Chesnutt's language here is suggestive, introducing one of the many aspects of the text that rely on "inference" rather than frank divulgence. Here in particular, he indicates that these assumptions about genealogy derived from clear physical evidence—the uncannily mirrored faces, for instance—can be "negatived," annulled by the racial "infusion" that exceeds epistemology. The strange grammar calls attention to the active process by which Blackness is deprived of being, converted to the vital nothingness against which whiteness defines itself. This is a world where nothing is what it seems, least of all destabilizing social and filial affairs. The blood relation suturing together this "strange couple" both exists and doesn't exist, as biology and power contradict one another's claims in this haunted landscape.

This emblematic twinning and absenting sets the tone for a plot hampered throughout by unspoken revelations, guarded secrets, mute admissions, and invisible knowledge. Murchison and Viney are once-master and once-slave who continue to live in indissoluble attachment decades after emancipation, although it is neither a peaceful nor a harmonious relationship but rather one beset by terrible violence and dependency. As a younger man, Murchison had set out to marry a local woman, but Viney in her "hysterical" fit of jealousy confronts the fiancée with a disastrous (but never explicitly disclosed) secret that destroys their marital plan. The unarticulated confession, which we are meant to "infer" as likely testimony to the family's racial transgressions evident in the blood and body of Viney herself, leads to a punishment that is also elliptically narrated but still palpably dreadful: Murchison beats Viney so mercilessly that she loses the ability to speak. She becomes the "dumb witness" of the story's title. Viney's muteness is advantageous to Murchison by safeguarding the secrets of the elite household, its perversions and its penalties. But the measure has unintended consequences for Murchison, who underestimates how intimately his own fate and status is yoked to Viney's. At about the same time, Murchison's uncle (the former owner of the plantation) dies, leaving Murchison the sole heir to the family property and fortune. However, the uncle hides the will and other documents attesting to Murchison's inheritance and rightful ownership. "I do not say here where they are," the uncle wrote in his farewell missive, "lest this letter might fall into the wrong hands; but your housekeeper Viney knows their hiding place. She is devoted to you and to the family—she ought to be, for *she is of our blood*— and she only knows the secret" (166, emphasis added).

With newfound compunction, Murchison thus attempts to nurse Viney back to health and restored capacity for communication. However, even when her "wound" is ostensibly "healed," every question he asks to determine the whereabouts of the papers is "answered in the negative" (168). She remains unable to speak clearly, and all attempts to teach her to write fail miserably. The mystery therefore remains with her, unable to be divulged either in language or body, despite her seeming "willing enough" (168). The only conclusion is that the secret, the legitimacy of mastery here, has disappeared into the "negative" space of the Black body that authorizes it and can never answer otherwise, never again to be seen or articulated. When the narrator arrives at the property many decades into the impasse, the now old man Murchison is still badgering Viney to give up the secret, or is "digging, digging furiously" in the yard, attempting to unearth the papers himself, while Viney watches with "inscrutable eyes" (170).

The Trees 39

The narrator concludes his business with the younger, saner, new master of the house, a nephew who seats the narrator in the oak chair the old man had just occupied. The chair itself serves as a metonym of the legacy of mastery, a "massive oak affair, with carved arms and back and a wooden seat, [which] looked as though it might be of ancient make, perhaps an heirloom" (161). Sitting here, in the furniture that both represents and conceals the literal, inherited "affair," the narrator seals the bargain for timber and leaves the property pleased. On the way out with his driver, Julius, he passes the elder Murchison, still "digging rapidly" in his "strange pursuit" (162)—indeed, another "strange" expedition into the fast tomb of earth and its unconfessed mysteries. Here, we also appreciate the terrible elision of Viney's Black body and the dark earth, both of which he attempts over and over again to penetrate for all it holds and withholds.

It is only after he leaves the property that the narrator learns the entirety of the saga from Julius; readers then, too, assemble the details of the mystery in real time, as it were. The final revelation for both does not come until the end of the tale, when the narrator returns to the property one year later with further business to conduct and finds the site markedly altered: new gate, new hinges; the grass, weeds, and shrubs are mowed and ordered. When he inquires about the improvements, Julius informs him that the mad old Murchison had died the month before, and that the younger Murchison is now the estate's owner. While half of the "strange couple" that haunted the front porch is now gone, the other—Viney— remains. Moreover, she addresses the visitor, revealing that her speech has been seemingly miraculously restored upon her tormentor's death. But Julius explains with "glee" that Viney had "never lost" her capacity to speak. She "could 'a' talked all de time, ef she'd had a min'ter." Too, she had always known exactly where the deed to the property had been hidden and had directed the new heir to the location: in the seat of the "ole oak a'm-cheer on de piazza yander" where the master had been sitting "all dese yeahs" (171). Furniture

40 *The Weird South*

with memories, indeed: the oak chair, the earth, and Viney all together, a consolidated force of sublimation containing and suppressing it all in plain sight and in ordered, mannered, perdurable silence.

I've related this story at some length not necessarily because it is singular, but because in many ways it is not. It is a narrative of secrecy and of poisonous greed, with a moral edge just barely legible for Reconstruction-era readers keen to appreciate the lessons of slavery with subtlety. Indeed, the discerning presence of the northern financier opens the vista just enough to spread the weight of reckoning with the ripples of a toxic economic engine, and the murkiness of the narrative couches much. Chesnutt's cleverness and his gravity are in making Viney appear to be the triumphant character: she outwits and outlives her victimizer, depriving him of the legal validation of his station on the basis of her own less legible but no less determining rights. Yet even though Murchison doesn't prosper materially in the end, neither does Viney. She has gained neither the property nor the integrity that might have been hers, absent that infusion of dark blood, and remains in servitude as ownership merely transfers to another set of white hands. The drama of Chesnutt's story is ultimately rather private, almost romantic: a revenge narrative with a meager but potent victory that is less about interfering with inalienable white proprietorship than it is about yielding to the perverse pleasures of shared alienation. That is to say, Murchison and Viney together constitute an uncanny dyad, a weird symmetry that far surpasses the master-slave relationship and renders it instead an organic expression of the inherently racialized southern family. The unit is infiltrated by the porousness of Black and white bodies in proximities of production, which in the story appears only obliquely to be sexual and more capaciously to signify a kind of ontological co-constitution.

Viney cannot leave this scene because she is integral to its structures. As her name suggests, a vine is a woody stem that doesn't grow or thrive independently but cleaves to structures

The Trees 41

and depends on their solidity to climb. Viney is the fleshy embodiment of the force that shrouds the house in obsolescence, and she is the chilling raw material for its resuscitation and continuance. The ruse of the buyer-narrator who comes to extract still more timber from a scene that has plenty yet to offer—the natural world continues to produce unchecked— alerts us to the endlessly regenerating structures of power that pass from one human entity to the next. The heir to the region's agronomic potential is now seated in the buggy of a northern vineyard owner who admits in the first paragraph that he "took advantage of [southerners] when [he] found it convenient and profitable to do so" (158). And yes, the narrator owns a *vine*yard just two miles away from the Murchison place, in the North Carolina sandhills. When he returns a year later, it is not simply that the Murchison place looks better but that it looks a lot more like his. As Julius reports, the new master "be'n ober to yo' place lookin' roun', an' he say he's gwinter hab his'n lookin' lak yi'n befo' de yeah's ober" (171).

Viney's haunting of this place, especially as it aspires to the grandeur of a vineyard, drives home the now more diffuse, extraregional, yet no less trenchant and controlling interests that persist in absorbing, transforming, and permanently detaining the raw elements in the southern web. Viney the ex-slave and violated other serves as the ur-Vine that both fortifies and persistently denies the legitimacy of the order that exploits her, passed from white hand to white hand to white hand. Viney's role is not parasitic but maybe paratactic, if you will: an alliance of parts that lose their capacity to exist in isolation but nonetheless strive for privacy and the silence of refusal.

Chesnutt's brilliance here, again, is in the way he encourages the reader, through veils of irony and unspoken implication, to confront a world irreversibly altered by rapacious needs—ecological, economic, erotic—all collapsed in a haunted architecture of codependency where no element can survive alone or with sovereignty, even and especially in demarcations of racial difference birthed by such rapacity. As if to underscore the enormity of this delusion, we are told at one point that Viney's racial mixture also includes "a dash of Indian blood," that prosaic sprinkle so often meted out in literary texts to help account or provide authority for a character's otherwise morally ambiguous actions. Here, the narrator suggests that this racial spice gives her straighter and darker hair, on the one hand—there's that optical proof again—but, more obliquely, "perhaps endowed her with some other qualities which found their natural expression in the course of subsequent events—if indeed her actions needed anything more than common human nature to account for them" (164). The phrase "common human nature" permits the very elemental empathy for Viney's victimization that animates the story, even as it slyly undercuts it, branding her as "common" and beset by undoing passions. The (again tacit) "other qualities" that Viney's Indigeneity lends are not clear, but we can guess that these are proclivities for subterfuge and vengeance, a primal deepening of her extraction potential sealed fast by her African blood. Her threat is metaphorical in the end, as she is little more than a vengeful ghost, a mute chair, a pruned vine, a dumb witness to the outrages of a bioeconomic order that endlessly reduplicates.

Here we should pause and reflect on what new vision of the South we are gaining with these capaciously materialist visions. As I suggested in the previous chapter, much of the critique of left-liberal, new materialist philosophies rests in their capitulation to the frustration of agency and moral culpability in the collapse of ontological difference. Slavoj Žižek's arresting thought experiment decomposes the Holocaust itself, rendering Auschwitz "an assemblage—in which the agents were not just the Nazi executioners but also the Jews, the complex network of trains, the gas ovens, the logistics of feeding the prisoners, separating and distributing clothes, extracting the gold teeth, collecting the hair and ashes and so on."[8] His point is that if everything has agency, then all things are responsible for atrocity and none has moral claim or opportunity to stop or reverse it. Worse, if there were any ethical sav-

The Trees 43

iors, they wouldn't be humans, given our track record. New materialist models, moreover, can become accidental allies of capitalism, obscuring the disastrous shaping power of social, institutional, and cultural norms under capitalist hegemonies, while insisting instead on the primary accountability of human narcissism: our lack of empathy for the moral integrity of other, "inferior" life forms.

What these approaches miss, of course, and what so much of this new critique hopes to reintroduce, are the historical conditions that shape reality, that ornament our language, our decisions, our taxonomies, our politics. What makes the Weird South so deeply illustrative and problematic in this regard is its concentration of such insights: that the natural world and inferior races exist in an assemblage of oversight and overdetermination; that historical forces have altered irrevocably the capacity for disambiguation, if not for regeneration; and that true liberation must occur within the spaces of detention—the structures, the furniture, the myriad "things" created out of the accumulation of victimhood. This is new materialism with a dark twist. It is a failure of ethical deliverance and yet simultaneously a critique of capitalist conversion with no romantic exits or alternative ways of being apart from its collapsed architecture.

So the Weird South asks us first to confront the completeness of the postplantation archive of transmutation and of decomposition, where bodies and materials are constrained by their co-constitution, where things and voices speak together in a garbled articulation. From there, we might plausibly attend to the smallest, most incremental acts of what Chesnutt styles as revenge, but what Monique Allewaert and some of the other critics I noted might call a strategic marshaling of the marginalized's alliance (both perceived and performed) with natural resources to effect punctuations of resistance and retaliation. Allewaert points frequently to the use among African slaves of Indigenous herbs and fetish objects derived from tribal cosmologies, which often allowed enslaved subjects to undertake resurgent acts of healing and regeneration.

These concepts reappear as generative devices and practices in, for example, Zora Neale Hurston's richly archival efforts to collect the animating cultural forms emerging from Black diasporic sites that she deems "the wombs of folk culture still heavy with life."[9] For Hurston, the proximity of Black, Creole, and Indigenous populations to the natural world provided a ready template for the organic creation of art steeped in indomitable traditions culled from African, Spanish, Native, and even English sites. The threatful capacity of such wombs emerges throughout African and Caribbean literary production as another signifier of continuity and connectivity. There is Édouard Glissant's concept of the archetypal slave ship as the "womb abyss": "It generates the clamor of your protests; it also produces all the coming unanimity. Although you are alone in this suffering, you share in the unknown with others whom you have yet to know. This boat is your womb, a matrix, and yet it expels you. This boat: pregnant with as many dead as living under sentence of death."[10]

Pregnant with possibility and with life forms and art, yet sentenced to death. We can't help but return here to the arrested and opened womb in Porter's story, and the dashed possibilities for generativity, cancelled by the boy (and incipient white Man) whose social and economic precarity compels administrative acts of violence against lesser creatures. What becomes possible in the subaltern experience of isolation and social death is a naturalistic hunger for relationality, for increase, for "unanimity" from the matrix of "your" making. "This is why we stay with poetry," Glissant suggests, "despite our consenting to all the indisputable technologies; despite seeing the political leap that must be managed, the horror of hunger and ignorance, torture and massacre to be conquered, the full load of knowledge to be tamed, the weight of every piece of machinery that we shall finally control, and the exhausting flashes as we pass from one era to another—from forest to city, from story to computer—at the bow [of the original boat] there is still something we now share: this murmur, cloud or rain or peaceful smoke. We know ourselves as part

The Trees 45

and as crowd, in an unknown that does not terrify . . . Our boats are open, and we sail them for everyone."[11] Glissant's contemporary perspective fills in what a writer like Chesnutt could only anticipate, as the rolling steam of machinery was transforming the old world of the South. The plantation demands, with all of the "indisputable technologies" and the burden of knowledge, "to be tamed," to be internalized, and the ongoing hungers and tortures of living in the interstices persist between a determinative past and a future of foreclosure. What Glissant calls poetry is really the appetite of the suppressed to continue speaking courageously into a crowd of solidarity, a coherence forged ironically in that primal womb of erasure, a shared experience of partiality that now unites. From forest to city, from trees to the architecture of loss: this movement threatens to eclipse these histories and the integrity of lives collapsed into the furniture of a social order that shifts imperceptibly from one means of production to the next, one inert commodity issued forth from the bodies and labor of the continually silenced, dumb witnesses and frustrated spectators to its evolution.

The insistence, whether in Chesnutt or Glissant or Allewaert or even Yaeger, on these minor acts of reunification is significant because it both acknowledges and rejects the incorporating logics of ecomaterialist determinism. In other words, these practices of resurgence plainly operate within spaces of entrapment and exile, despite and because of the wholesale decomposition of the managed body into the machinery of progress. Transformed, truncated, and voided, they yet erupt formidably with these reminders of encounter. With "cloud or rain or peaceful smoke," those frail forms emergent at the womb of chattel becoming, which are just "murmurs"—poetry, really, snapshots rather than long-form exegesis. And they are, importantly, part of the natural world that both preexists and survives such outrage—raw materials for a new becoming, one forged in peaceful surrender rather than violent annihilation. It is just this kind of quiet infiltration into the fabric of technology broadly construed that forms the basis

46   *The Weird South*

for much science fiction and speculative literature, a huge subgenre of which belongs to African American and Indigenous authors, not incidentally. As Deleuze and Guattari put it, in language remarkably similar to Glissant's: in attending to the assemblages of postmodernity that include machines but only as contingent components of a vast, rhizomatic reality, we must listen carefully for "the sound of a contiguous future, the murmur of new assemblages of desire, of machines, and of statements, that insert themselves into the old assemblages and break them."[12]

These are utopian visions, in some ways, born from the dread of annihilation. And while the expectant levitation in this trajectory is a place to which we want and need to ascend, I think the waypoints offered by the Weird South offer arresting apertures into the dark web of things, into the poverties of integrity left after the leveling of assemblages. They entreat us to reckon with the unavailability of some kinds of contiguity in systems of rupture, alienation, and dehumanization, or the stymying self-symmetry of the once-enslaved and contemporary machine. It is a delicate forensics, to be sure, and one dramatized by the anchoring physics of trauma in sites like the plantation South. What these weird southern ontologies encourage us to see simultaneously are the place-bound ravages of ecomaterialist embeddedness within racial-capitalist economies, alongside the invitations to conceptualize personhood by logics instilled in deep time rather than in Anthropocenic coordinates, and in modes beyond the technology of the pen or the computer or even the strictly literary.[13] In such archives, a dumb witness and a static chair may in fact be the most revelatory conduits to the knowledge compressed in the biotic environment and its mutated forms, ancient and enigmatic.

But in posing such possibilities and such eruptions, we tread closely to a landscape of potential romance that I want to challenge in the next chapter, where we entertain the seductions of Indigenous lifeways as countertropes to the haunting architecture of the unthought knowns and of human-centered

The Trees 47

calamity. Here, I want to dwell just a bit more intently on the ontological prison fashioned for African subjects in particular in and by a postplantation world that fails to jettison its coordinates of meaning-making. To do so, I want to turn briefly to one of the most powerful voices in this regard in twentieth-century African American literature: Richard Wright.

Wright's work is currently undergoing a major reevaluation inspired by the 2021 publication of *The Man Who Lived Underground*, a novel that he had finished at the conclusion of the Depression but that remained unpublished in his lifetime, likely because of its horrific depictions of racism and police brutality. A much-reduced version had appeared in Wright's posthumous collection *Eight Men* (1961), but the full-length novel was lost to literary history until his daughter Julia instigated its recent publication.[14] Wright finished the novel in 1942; he left the Communist party in 1944 and fled America permanently shortly after World War II, spending the remainder of his life as an expatriate in France. Wright's searing critiques of American racism and political economy are well known, so canonized are the relentlessly bleak *Native Son* (1940) and his autobiography *Black Boy* (1945), which captures the frank horrors of growing up in rural, Jim Crow Mississippi. He had arrived in Chicago along with his family in the late 1920s (an odyssey rendered in the longer version of his memoir, *American Hunger*, which was not restored to the original and published in full form until 1977) and spent the Depression years involved in Communist politics and publishing his early protest fiction and essays. The most notable of these early efforts are *Uncle Tom's Children* (1938), a collection of short fiction set in the South, and the rhapsodic *12 Million Black Voices* (1941), a quasi-journalistic response to the Farm Security Administration's teeming photographic archive of Black migrants. In this latter work, Wright carefully captions photographs of Black subjects on southern plantations and in urban spaces and amplifies them with his own detailed narrative of the brutal chronicles of chattel slavery in the American South—essentially giving not just "voices" but

48 *The Weird South*

also deep, unsparing histories to the silent images that otherwise were left to viewers' interpretation or disregard. David Bradley identifies the result as anomalous in Wright's career, calling it "a work of poetry, of passion, of lyricism and of love."[15] While tender at times, *12 Million Black Voices* as a whole is nonetheless a bitter exercise in witness: a precipitous reckoning with settler-colonial history that highlights the alienation of the Black body in a strange, Western land, and continues through the violent chronicles of slavery, migration, and annihilation in the markets and materials of American industry. But throughout, Wright's strategy is to locate the essential, binding humanity "beneath the garb of the black laborer." Far from static or stable, the experience of the Black worker constitutes "an uneasily tied knot of pain and hope whose snarled strands converge from many points of time and space."[16]

Those "snarled strands" and "many points of time and space" beguile elliptically, conjuring an American experience that, for all its intense and undeniable suffering, is somehow diffuse, twisted, and unmappable. While he accounts incisively for the persistence of the plantation structures that once enslaved his ancestors, he also identifies an ethereal incentive that is entirely beyond labor and its paltry recompense. "Trapped," he writes, ". . . we beg bread of the Lords of the Land and they give it to us . . . We plow, plant, chop, and pick the cotton, working always toward a dark, mercurial goal."[17] What was already a crisis of value for all Americans becomes an existential guttering for free Black workers: to be both valued and expunged, exploited and superseded, rooted and unlocatable. In turn, and following Wright's own trajectory, the most chilling images in the book are set not in the cotton South but in urban despair. Children sleep in groups on tenement floors or huddle under overpasses. Men toil, filthy, in dark underground spaces. Perhaps most affecting, large families gaze up with expectant faces, clearly hungering for the best, or come together with hands raised in prayer or bodies alive with dance. Wright expertly juxtaposes these visions of

The Trees   49

anguish and anticipation, ending with a grave recital not of Blacks' irrelevance but of their agency. Here there is a brief optimism forged in the crucible of Depression activism when white workers admitted their Black peers into unions, to stand together rather than fall separately. In the end, Wright's message is one of complicated hope: as Black families struggle forth with the rest of America, he sees them both "moving!" along with others, even though, ultimately, "we pay in the coin of death."[18]

While the inter- and cross-racial activism of the decade forged new solidarity in some quarters, and New Deal programs helped some Black families inch toward improved circumstances, Wright is attuned more and more to the concatenating historical trauma that would not yield in the face of freedom or recovery—with an increasingly vague, "mercurial" payoff. This pessimism is understandably muted in *12 Million Black Voices*, a work of vaguely propagandistic social commentary, but erupts forcefully in *The Man Who Lived Underground*, which he wrote shortly after. The story is based loosely on a true crime story from the 1930s and is marked emphatically by the dark mood and murkiness of the decade. Yet, precisely because of migration and the Depression's vertiginous unmoorings, he refuses to anchor the narrative to explicit chronological or geographic coordinates. Paula Rabinowitz limns the subtle ways in which Depression-era literature is replete with such discombobulation in its preoccupation with "tropes of positioning, of location, of place, or rather, of displacement, derailment, missing locations, and missed connections. Spatial order—central to demarking borders between industrial and residential zones, between men and women, between workers and their bosses, between races, between parents and their children—while sharply visible, still tangibly in effect, could no longer be counted on to signify as they once had."[19] Rocked by detonations of stability in this newly leveled landscape—no longer certain where one is, and in relation to what or to whom—the reliability of identity and filial markers deteriorates.

50   *The Weird South*

Like the city streets in *12 Million Black Voices*, the setting of the novella and its protagonist occupy a harrowing space between the plantation and the city, slavery and freedom, the coin of opportunity and of social death. The plot, in brief, involves a Black laborer named Fred Daniels who is wrongfully accused of murdering a white couple, is tortured by the police, and is finally brutalized into a confession. He manages to escape into the city's underground sewer system, but his "freedom" comes at the cost of any remaining vestiges of his humanity. Wright's depictions of Fred being tortured by the police in the opening sections—available to readers for the first time in the 2021 edition—are sickeningly proleptic, presaging the atrocities that American Black men and women have for decades suffered at the hands of white officers. One particularly revolting scene describes a parched Fred, hours into his interrogation, being offered a drink of water, only to have the liquid violently expelled from his body at the instant he begins to swallow. "Perfect!" one officer exclaims, "I heard the water squish!" (18). The dreadful physicality of such scenes contrasts starkly with the story's underground opacity, where Fred quickly loses all worldly coordinates; almost immediately, "time stood still" there (65). Even before he slips underground, his extended torture removes him from any stable sense of time or space and leaves him "yearning for oblivion" (26). To some extent, he receives his abuse in the liminal space between the white world above and the dark obscurity below, between waking and dreaming, incarceration and emancipation.

It is a race nightmare, to be sure, but one that Wright seems able to render only slant, through the metrics of money and materiality that Fred jettisons along with his innocence. This conception of "oblivion" just barely precedes the Heideggerian notion, set forth in the latter's 1946 "Letter on Humanism," wherein the existential beingness of humans falters threatfully in the face of the modern ascendance of technology, among other safeguards of sovereignty. The "yearning" for this state, in turn, is an indicator of moderni-

The Trees 51

ty's fatal wear on its subjects, and the novella charts this odyssey. The story opens on payday, as Fred leaves his job in a white neighborhood, counting the "slender roll of green bills clutched in his right fist." He is fatigued but briefly "happy," aware of having "given his bodily strength in exchange for dollars with which to buy bread and rent for the coming week," and transfers the hard-won cash from his tight fist to his pocket "so that he would run no risk of losing it."[20] The "slender" compensation sits in arrears to his actual labor—he muses on how sore his hand is from the week's mowing—and promises only the barest subsistence. But Fred literally clings to the "exchange." What he loses, immediately upon safeguarding his cash, is his freedom: he is accosted by the police who believe he fits the description of the alleged murderer. After being systematically tortured for hours, Fred is finally taken back to his apartment to see his laboring wife (the metaphor does not escape us). Finding her in acute distress, the officers grudgingly transport her to the hospital and in the process briefly relax custody of Fred. The terrified man seizes the opportunity to disappear through a manhole and into the underground sewer system. *Underground*, again.

Freedom, Wright suggests, is a bargain made with the coin of death, a trope evident in the postplantation labor economy but legible only in the bowels of the urban marketplace. Here Fred must shed the trappings of modernity in order to see its operations plainly—literally observing the action in a movie theater, a Black church, an undertaker's chamber, a jewelry store, a meat market, and a fruit store. His spectrality also grants him free access to material possessions. He steals a worker's lunchbox and a handgun, acquires a radio and a typewriter and a meat cleaver, and unlocks a safe and pilfers stacks of cash, watches, and diamonds. He learns the combination to the safe by watching a "white hand" scroll through the combination over and over; his own dark hand mimics the code, as it were, and unlocks a bounty that dwarfs the "slender roll" he had earlier clutched. But away from the aboveground marketplace, the haul is detached from any fis-

52 *The Weird South*

cal standard, a mere mockery of value. He unwraps the stacks of bills and reads their imprint with a "musing laugh," with "no desire to count the money; it was what it stood for—all the manifold currents of life swirling aboveground—that captivated him" (94). The coin of death, the currency of life—it amounts to the same. He pastes the money to the wall of his cave as a "mocking symbol" to the world that had exploited him and becomes hysterical at the contrast: "He remembered how he had hugged the few dollars" he had earned, and now this: "He was *free!*" (95–96).

Fred's hideout is festooned with the other stolen symbols of his liberty—money and machines and weapons in suggestive proximity—and he struggles to understand their effect on him. Possessed almost mystically by a "weird feeling" in the "strange land" of his new life, he grows fearful but also complacent, surrendering to the "bizarre and ghostly" aura of modernity's artifacts and their violence (109–10). Importantly, rather than alienate, they enliven him to the experience of a broader human collective. Here again, the "weird" and the "strange" present portals to the fatal entanglements of modernity but also to a perverse sense of community: "They seemed to stand for events that had happened in another life," and he believes "that the true identity of these forces would slowly reveal themselves, not only to him but also to others" (108–9). Fred suffers the epiphany that "he was *all people . . .* and they were *he . . .* this was the oneness that linked man to man," while still clinging to the dawning recognition of "the inexpressible value and importance of himself" (106–7). In the limbo of expectancy, Fred's "value" and self are tangled up with the collection of symbols in his cave. He is a victim of the meat cleaver. His name he can recall only by tapping it awkwardly on a typewriter "machine"—a "queer instrument, something beyond the rim of his life"; and yet, it is in this metal box that the secret of his identity is trapped (91).

Wright wants us to understand the poverty of freedom and the haunting chimera of Fred's faith as conditions not just of racial subjugation but of modernity's disillusions and

The Trees 53

of economic collapse. While Wright declared *The Man Who Lived Underground* most autobiographical work,[21] he also remarked in a letter to his publisher that, perhaps surprisingly, it was "the first time I've really tried to step beyond the straight black-white stuff."[22] But what exactly does he mean by this? In the explanatory essay he wrote to accompany the novel, Wright documents his efforts to critique his grandmother's religious faith, and by extension that of "Negroes" of a certain generation and class who clung to their belief in things unseen, an irrepressible hope "outside time and space" that left them "*in* this world but not *of* this world."[23] But which world is this? This gutter of oblivion captures, in many ways, the otherworld that Wright creates for Fred, and it is both the raced and the raceless detention of modernity. Fred's loss is thus both existential and ontological: inside and outside, aboveground and below, his inability to be reified or fulfilled is an index of modernity's evacuations and faith's dissembling substitutes.

To express the intimacy of the "black-white" plight with the empty promises of the spiritual and secular marketplaces, Wright depicts a form of physical hunger that Fred cannot satisfy. He shows the man devouring an undigestible amount of food: two large pork sandwiches (he ingests even the bones, "like a dog"), an apple, three pears, two bananas, several oranges, and heavy gulps of water "until his stomach seemed about to burst" (78, 115). Wright had dabbled in food and lifestyle writing for the WPA during the Depression, and as Colleen Glenney Boggs demonstrates, he continued to write vividly about food and hunger in his later work, often in sharp critique of other Black writers whose interest in foodways indulged more romantically in folk culture. Wright instead tends to bind labor to physical hunger in order to descry the racial stereotype, and perverse residues, of "white generosity and Black greed."[24] As Boggs points out, Wright's portrayals of hunger are not simply symbolic, as many critics have assumed, but expressions of "real, material deprivation" that he himself experienced and shares with his characters.[25] Of

54   *The Weird South*

course, they are both, and he suggests here that the material and the affective are indissolubly bound. Desperate, bottomless need exceeds sustenance and logic and becomes pure, unquenchable desire. Scenes of Fred's ravenous consumption are thus detailed erotically: Fred "sucking the core" of an apple, emitting an orgasmic "groan," and falling asleep to dream about a nude woman and baby in distress, a nightmare from which he wakes alarmed and "erect" (78–80). Unmistakably, Wright wants us to see Fred both seduced and unnerved by his attempts to join all of humanity at the communal table of longing and denunciation, leading us to feel the insatiable hunger for a never-sufficient feast of modernity's offerings, to hear the water squeak, as it were, fountaining sickeningly out of the bodies wracked by history and modernity's reiterative abuses.

"This isn't the doctrinal Wright," Imani Perry observes, "warning us of the disasters that capitalism creates. It's the unmooring Wright, pushing us past the edge of social analysis and into madness."[26] What if "madness" is understood, in this case, as a function of the weird—a way of exceeding the usual terms and measures of social analysis, "unmooring" us entirely from the coordinates of the made world where men like Fred suffer? Because of the hyperbole of the narrative, its excessive brutality and suffering, we might miss the profundity of Wright's materialist critique. In the end, the "madness" he paints is the relentless deprivation and continuities of postplantation, post-emancipation, post-Depression existence. After stealing into and gorging himself within what he believes is a closed shop, a woman and companion come in looking to buy grapes. Fred scrambles silently to play the role of clerk. "You'd better give me a pound of the dark ones," the woman says, her locution unduly threatening for the occasion, and Fred hands her a too-large bunch—"that's more than a pound, isn't it?" she remarks (116–17). A modern Shylock demanding in dark flesh the repayment of a loan, the woman's demand triggers the story's most profound insight: that of the Black body as a limitless field of extraction, once

The Trees 55

legally bound by slavery and Jim Crow and, in the mockery of freedom, still coerced, detained, determined, and consumed by forces of law, administration, and commerce. The woman places a dime in his hand, a meager exchange, but after she leaves he flings it to the ground. Refusing the "coin of death" is another gesture of estrangement from the modern meat market but also from the seductions of such emancipation.

In this moment, Fred has the overwhelming sense that "though the underground claimed him, it rejected him" too, and knows "he could not stay" (118). Yet there is nowhere for him to go, because, whether aboveground or below, he is always both anywhere and everywhere, an everyman and a nobody much like the condition of Heideggerian, metaphysical oblivion, the *unheimlich* modern, the Freudian uncanny, the Bhabhaian unhomely. The buffet of philosophical concepts is limitless but also limited. What Wright tells us ultimately is a tale of unifying emotional suffering with deep historical roots and "snarled" modern afterlives, a totalizing condition that allows no escape or exit. None of the glittering things he gains have use value in this underground space, where he tacks his collection up like wallpaper—a useless fetish. His triumphant knowledge, like Viney's, affirms rather than releases him from the made world's logics and violence. At one moment he stands drenched in sweat from laboring ceaselessly in the dark to assemble this collection of insights and things and begins "brooding about the diamonds, the rings, the watches, the money; he remembered the singing in the church, the people yelling in the movie, the dead baby, the nude man stretched out upon the table . . . He saw these items hovering before his eyes and felt that some dim meaning linked them together, that some magical relationship made them kin . . . [and that] they were striving to tell him something" (51).

It is this kinship—this magical relationship that collapses the distinction between "items"—that both conjures an animistic, pre-settler-colonial, preracial capitalist assemblage of forms, bodies, humanity, and hope and renders them all things, stripped externally and internally, nude and evacu-

56 *The Weird South*

ated, empty of integrity. He is both free and eternally imprisoned. His cave is both a "mocking symbol" and a wasteland. Unseen by the surveillance of the white world, he has stolen nothing, he "had simply picked it up, just as a man would pick up firewood in a forest." But we know that such discoveries, in the settler-colonial chronicle, are never just that, that "finding firewood" means forcefully eviscerating trees and forests and people. What Fred Daniels now experiences is the epiphanic ontological endpoint of that same story. The world aboveground now seemed to him "a wild forest filled with death" (54). But the underground is no precolonial haven, no magical reunion with a landscape of disambiguated parts, no place where everything is not always already owned. Its potentiality merges uncannily with the savagery laid bare, the wild forest that always was and always is concealed beneath the surface of things.

In the end, in a fit of both intrepidness and insanity, Fred returns aboveground eager to share all that he has learned and delusional about what such "freedom" might promise, only to be shot dead by the police and returned to the sewer, "a whirling, black object . . . lost in the heart of the earth."[27] He is "lost" either way, a formless representative of all Black men and all humanity at once, moving in astonishment between states of recognition and befuddlement, kinship and isolation, community and rejection. In this space of loss, we sense something of Wright's compulsion to move beyond the "black-white stuff" in his expansive vision of collective trauma, both the prospect and the despair of being released from administration, coercion, and control. Such oblivion is alternately demanded and foreclosed by modernity and the lessons of the Depression, which eradicate and ossify difference all at once and in turn. Fred's knowledge that his own value can be insisted upon only in concert with the demystification of modernity's elusive symbols is astute: the two are yoked, embedded in particularly corrosive histories that sustain fictions of difference hinging precisely on those mystifications of power. Placing Wright's postplantation cri-

The Trees 57

tiques in the post-Depression oblivion urges us beyond our own continued insistence on locating and labeling trauma as distinctive rather than—or at the same time that it is—shared, even "snarled." As we see in the end of Wright's narrative, death becomes a startling alternative to the adherences of modernity and the divisive polarities of Depression fatigue. But there, oblivion signifies also as an entry into the implosive wilderness beyond, both real and imagined. The compelling environment of anticapitalist purity and tribalism gains heightened appeal during periods of economic emergency and is the subject of the next and final chapter here.

In many ways, Wright's story is a predictor for the increasingly stark, bleak works of African American fiction that would follow and that we don't have time to do justice to here. But as a harbinger of the comprehensive despair, the nihilism that has saturated so much of the literary and scholarly operations of antiblack critique, it is profoundly revealing. For our purposes in these chapters, where we are poised at a critical juncture between reading for trauma and reading for deliverance, we are hard-pressed to locate the latter in a world that has so steadily altered and scripted every opportunity for such awakenings, reunifications, and grace. To be lost in the heart of the earth is at the same time to sink into a cradle, but is it a movement of resignation or of return? Can it be both at once? I think it can and must be, if we are to survive with a semblance of optimism for an as-yet-untold future, and it seems to me the lesson of these weird southern orientations is that we embrace the friction of such dualism. It is possible for such hope to extend too far, into a space of fantasy that does little work to limn the fractures of loss, before attempting to mend them and before arriving at a sober assessment of what remains to be repaired. That is where we'll go in the final chapter.

For now, I want to end with an image from another ending, that of Jesmyn Ward's 2017 novel, *Sing, Unburied, Sing*, the devastating follow-up to her National Book Award–winning *Salvage the Bones*.[28] There is so much to say about this haunt-

58 *The Weird South*

ing book, but to close this reverie on trees I want to pause briefly on a moment at the novel's close. The protagonist—a sensitive adolescent boy named Jojo—finally witnesses the raw, overwhelming manifestation of the ghost world he has sensed and channeled throughout the book's sober events. He has just returned from a harrowing trip to Parchman Prison with his mother, a drug addict, and his baby sister, who is ill and vomits uncontrollably during the entire trip. They go to pick up the children's father, who has been incarcerated there, but they also return home with a decades-passed ghost of another inmate, a young thirteen-year-old boy like Jojo himself, whose experience overlaps with that of Jojo's family and encapsulates the strange mutations of southern horror as it trickles through the twentieth century and beyond. This ghost huddles on the floor of the car, among the "crumpled pieces of paper and plastic" (141) and the vomit, a "boy on the floor sinking farther down" (169) into the detritus of southern modernity, a mirror for Jojo's hopes. Back at the family's house, the ghost retreats further into the crawl space beneath, in "the dirt under the living room where they all sleep, making a cot of the earth. . . . And [singing] songs without words."

The wordless, ineffable songs of the ghost from this sunken place stretch backward in time to contain the primordial beginning of the end for African chattel in the new world,[29] evoking long expanses of water breaking onto land, yurts and teepees and villages giving way to cities and skyscrapers, and full of people—alone and together, working, swimming, disappearing into buildings, and singing constantly with their bodies rather than their mouths. "It comes from the black earth and the trees and the ever-lit sky," Jojo tells us, "the most beautiful song I have ever heard, but I can't understand a word" (241). Perhaps this is the most apt note to end on, this impression of how haunting might give way to the capaciousness of vision and articulation that emerges from earth, tree, and sky as one, that bodes a collective consciousness and a hymn of the body that moves fluidly between history and now, between erasure and existence, unintelligible in any lexi-

The Trees 59

con we know, and yet inimitably "beautiful" despite and perhaps because of its untranslatability. Perhaps this is as far as we can come.

The novel ends not in this pregnant underbelly, but with the ghost emerging from underground to show Jojo the legion other spirits who share space with the living, who simmer and sing in the earth and the trees. "So many of us," he says. "So many crying loose. Lost. . . . Now you understand life." And then Jojo sees it: the ghost "ascends the tree . . . undulates along the trunk, to the branches, where he rolls out along one . . . And the branches are full. They are full with ghosts, two or three, all the way up to the top, to the feathered leaves. There are women and men and boys and girls. Some of them near to babies . . . They perch like birds, but look as people" (282). They speak with their eyes to Jojo about the horrors of their suffering and death. Jojo absorbs it all, their endless songs of sorrow which somehow become one in the air, an affirmation, a simple "*Yes*" (283). "I stand," Jojo says, "until the forest is a black-knuckled multitude" (282).

CHAPTER 3

The Forest

I want to begin by returning to the end of the previous chapter, where Jesmyn Ward's visionary narrator leaves us in a liminal space between the living and the dead, between trauma and regeneration, between alienation and a collective will to endure and to express, albeit in forms we may be unable to register, to witness, or to comprehend. This "forest [that] is a black-knuckled multitude" is a formidable idea, to be sure, and an inversion of the usual colloquialism: to "white-knuckle" means to "endure (an event or experience) which provokes fear, suspense, or anxiety," and specifically, "to grip (something) so tightly through fear or tension that one's knuckles whiten."[1] Retouched here, the Black multitudes and the trees keen together, sutured collectively despite unimaginable loss and rupture. In the grip of suffering, the trees become forest again, a metaphor for return, reclamation, regeneration. The multitude leans together when individual trees, branches, lives are cut down, absorbed into a voracious economy of signification that has brutalized land, bodies, identities, and our methods for reckoning. Now, in a moment of clear ecological emergency, we need to reckon not just with the tyranny of human-centered rapaciousness but with its totalizing, self-annihilating effects—its damning capacity to permanently scramble the parts: subhuman, parahuman,

61

not-human, vegetable, animal, mineral, Indian chief . . . Not surprisingly, we need to radically jettison the phantom of a "human" that exceeds any of these parts, any conception thereof that is not vitally entangled with all of it, any version of the idea that attempts to furiously disambiguate itself with axes, shovels, and increasingly sophisticated tools of order, control, meaning, and wealth making. We need to travel back to the forest.

This journey, as you might imagine, is not without landmines. There are gaping holes in the earth, if you will, places to sink and become trapped, for knowledge and evidence and bodies to lodge and fester. Perhaps the primary red herring here (and yes, I again use that phrase deliberately) is the trope of Indigeneity as conceptual counterpoise or historical-political-cultural antidote to the bankruptcy of modern human agency through imaginative returns to precolonial, precapitalist and antimodern idylls or spiritual systems as irresistible gateways. This impulse is pervasive and well documented as a feature of white settler-colonial anxiety and guilt, and it has plagued southern literature uniquely, more than any other regional mode in the United States, for reasons we have already begun to explicate. These yearnings come from both Indigenous and non-Indigenous perspectives, which are differently but not differentially significant; that is to say, there is no logical way to disambiguate or privilege essential, exclusive, or exceptional identity forms when those partitions have been manufactured by the very systems we're trying to escape. More specifically, as I've argued elsewhere, an "Indian" does not exist apart from the settler economies of its production as a concept and colonial placeholder, just as the slave *as such* does not preexist its function within the plantation machinery. The Indian, therefore, exists plausibly now as a retroactive device, a romance of origins that might deliver us. But despite the reiterative logics of this process, and all its damaging returns, there is still much to learn from the kernel of Weird Indigeneity that both lives and outlives the mythology. Weird Indigeneity entreats us to see the always-partial nature with which humans might imagine their implication in the biosphere, the uncanny ruptures and haunted spaces that can't be simply restored by sweeping myths of "sustainability" or undifferentiated celebrations of a posthuman assemblage. So, this final chapter poses something of an experimental journey: a map to a weird, new place.

To begin, let's return to the foundational concept of the "weird," which we can now finesse a bit after our work in the previous chapters. For Morton, again, arriving at a functional embrace of weird reality means excluding nothing from the web of what he calls the "implosive whole" or "symbiotic real."[2] We have seen how unflinchingly southern literary production labors, from a number of different impulsive, compulsive, and propulsive places, to unveil this knowledge in all its uncanny horror, and how its characters burrow into graves and sewers and crawl spaces in order to access its complicated, undoing potential. None of it has been plainly revelatory or redemptive, but there is repair in the glimpses afforded to them and to us. It should be clear by now that I am deeply skeptical of the reparative mode, to which much feminist, antiracist, and decolonial critique aspires, as a strategy for healing trauma or confronting division.[3] Moreover, we have been encouraged urgently in these southern contexts to be cautious about indulging in fantasies of redemption via the appealing features of biotic solidarity; we are seduced but not finally satisfied by intimations of romanticized reunions with natural and nonhuman otherworlds. Even an initially innocuous recognition of the bacterial passengers that live within and outside our bodies, marking our inherent occupation and permeability, has unnerving consequences. These are not chummy roommates that any of us can look at the same way after COVID, to be sure, and they point broadly to the vulnerability of our human organism as we surrender to its subscendent reality. Indeed, posthuman admissions inevitably slip from romantic exercises to threats to human sovereignty, made even more explosive when we confront the vastly different vulnerabilities of disparate bodies trapped within inequitable bio-

The Forest 63

political regimes, haunted by the inalterable species adaptations of settler-colonial and racial-capitalist histories. We are fundamentally different now. There is no primal *Anthropos* in the Anthropocene. We are entangled in messy, inextricable ways with the products and the victims and the mechanisms of our suffering, which makes any escape, alternative, or liberal-ethical plan of action or politics of repair seem puerile at best.

But this would be an unacceptable place to end either this book or our hopes for a world and its aggregate species desperate for relief. To even begin to imagine a truly leveled, correlationist, antiracist world emerging eventually from the broadscale deprecations of entwined economic and ecological tragedy, we need to do more of what we have been doing throughout these pages: to pause, first and foremost, over the distorted scales of witness and to diagnose the uneven degrees of culpability and affect meted to different subjects made possible precisely by these elisions. That is, as we saw in the previous chapter, we must expose our inherent affinity for biotic worlds as a materially dissimilar phenomenon for white and Black inhabitants of this nation and of the South, and as I want to suggest briefly here, something still more distinctive for Indigenous cultures. Morton's contribution, building on work by a number of influential theorists and philosophers from a span of disciplines—an intellectual aggregate that performs the very work it espouses—helps us to understand deeper, more haunting tissues of connectivity that do not tend necessarily toward wholeness or completion but hinge on absence, gaps, spectrality, and the unknown. As David Graeber puts it, when we engage in mystifications about Indigenous cultures, we often do so as an "ethical imperative" or reflex that demonstrates "respect for [Indigenous] otherness"; but in doing so, true solidarity is threatened, and we fail to acknowledge "one of the most important things all humans really do have in common: the fact that we all have to come to grips, to one degree or another, with *what we cannot know*."[4] Indeed, elemental to the concept of weirdness is the understanding that we can never fully understand it in isolated snatches but only collectively, implosively, and spectrally.

And yet, given the urgency of all this, the impulses to return to Indigenous perspectives, philosophies, and practices as vital alternatives to the apocalyptic conditions of climate disaster and its biopolitical comorbidities have been plainly seductive and remarkably difficult to dislodge or even to critique. As Arundhati Roy puts it, "the first step toward reimagining a world gone terribly wrong would be to stop the annihilation of those who have a different imagination"[5]—a modest proposition, indeed. More than simply "stopping the annihilation," scholars are increasingly invoking the imaginative and practical reservoirs of Indigenous knowledge for what they might offer that "world gone terribly wrong." Many scholars have turned seriously to non-Western cultures more broadly, seeking to learn from their seemingly privileged access to nonhuman and natural lifeworlds and to uniquely constructive practices of radical sustainability, grounded normativity, ontological connectedness, and interspecies kinship as lifelines to a more just ecological future. This shift has come in many theoretical guises, which we call variously the ontological turn, object-oriented ontology, new materialism, and posthumanism, building on foundational thinking elaborated by Michel Foucault, Deleuze and Guattari, Bruno Latour, Elizabeth Povinelli, Graham Harman, Timothy Morton, Donna Haraway, Sylvia Wynter, Anna Tsing, and others—a collective effort to level the hierarchical distinctions between human, nonhuman, and "natural" inhabitants of the biosphere. These turns have produced a range of relational concepts about leveled and imbricated "landscapes" (Gan et al.), "making kin" and "Chthulucene" (Haraway), ethical "mutualism" (Rose), "entangled spaces" (Farrier), and an "implosive whole" or "symbiotic real" (Morton).[6] Many of these formulations build explicitly on Indigenous cultural knowledge, sometimes without formally crediting those sources, as Sarah Hunt, Zoe Todd, and others have contended.[7] Some Indigenous thinkers themselves have entered traditional phenomenologies and material

The Forest 65

practices into mainstream scientific discourse fruitfully, such as the Indigenous Climate Change Studies movement facilitated by Potawatomi scientist Kyle Whyte. In a range of cli-fi works and other speculative narratives about the hypothetical survival of humankind, Indians are frequently the lifelines. Take, for example, Bong Joon-hoo's apocalyptic climate thriller *Snowpiercer*, in which Earth's two sole survivors are an Inuit girl and an African American boy, symbolic vestiges destined to "spread the human race."[8] Similarly, in *The Mermaids, or Aiden in Wonderland* (2018), a recent short film by the influential anthropologist Elizabeth Povinelli, we encounter a near future where "the world is being poisoned and Europeans are unable to step outside, while *Indigenous people are able to.*"[9] In other words, Indigenous epistemologies and politics are having a moment.

While many Indigenous approaches do offer pertinent, beneficent measures, they are often hindered by important recognitions of cultural disparities that apportion blame and salvation differently according to the differential logics and politics of settler-colonial repair. The broadscale characterization and application of Indigenous practices as exceptional in this regard have the effect of depositing fresh essentialisms in the wake of the old. As a result, the very incommensurability that these new approaches seek to demolish—those nourished by the imperial practices we aim to counter[10]—are rejuvenated in perdurable ways. Stuart Hall explains these New World mystifications as a direct function of the settler-colonial utopia, which, because it "is constituted for us as place, a narrative of displacement," engenders an "imaginary plenitude, recreating the endless desire to return to 'lost origins,' to be one again with the mother, to go back to the beginning." But, like the Lacanian imaginary, such returns yield no fulfillment but only the perpetuation of "the symbolic, of representation, the infinitely renewable source of desire, memory, myth, search, discovery."[11] No symbolic mother is more compelling than the entwined mythology of mother Earth and the forsaken Indigenous, a twin longing and source of desire that has

66   *The Weird South*

plagued American consciousness since its colonial origins and that redoubles now in our not-quite-but-trying-to-get-there "post"-colonial awakening. As critic Annie Olaloku-Teriba similarly explains, race is often conjured in such contexts "not as an anchor, but as a mystification conjured to weather crises of legitimacy"[12]—and, we must add, as a romance permanently indentured to the very operations that threaten the endurance of the earth and all who inhabit it. Indeed, the demarcations of race and identity grow more durable over time, and yet the conditions and consequences of their institution beg us to confront analogy rather than alterity, connection rather than fracture.

Thinking more seriously about the tangled materialities of the Anthropocene has permitted literary scholars in particular to better apprehend the textured phenomena of modernity: one where production and consumption imbue interior landscapes and unsettle divisive ontologies; where objects and goods occupy central space in the cultural imaginary and our affective ecologies; where the human, natural, and built worlds overlay in unruly, disruptive ways; and where the tyranny of the human subject collapses into a broader network of interconnection that imperils the hoary axioms of civilization itself.[13] In response to these irrefutable conditions, works produced in the postplantation South especially tend to feature complicated rejections of both material and discrete racial identification systems that no longer serve or sustain. Acknowledging the vast interconnectedness of both natural and manufactured life, the modern southern body wakens to its imbrication and unreality simultaneously, no longer secured by the anchors of race and apartheid and agrilogistical measures. The kind of vivid, literal hunger and unquenchable desire suffered by Wright's underground protagonist emblematizes this loss, as does the recognition of his etiology within a system of increasingly opaque cruelty that never disappears—Adam Smith's "invisible hand" grown ever more spectral and wounding all at once.[14] As we see in the end of Wright's narrative, death becomes a startling alternative to

The Forest 67

the adherences of modernity and its divisive polarities. But there oblivion also signifies an entry into the implosive "wilderness" beyond, both real and imagined: death as wilderness, as a compelling environment of anticapitalist purity and tribalism that gains heightened appeal during periods of economic emergency.

As one salient example of the simultaneous allure and repulsion of this "wilderness" and all it conjures about settler-colonial history and racial capitalism, Indigenous representations and motifs gained special purchase in the twentieth century and beyond. As Walter Benn Michaels and others have explored, the natural "Indian" emerges as a compensatory symbol in the writings of the most influential authors of the period.[15] Once portrayed as noble or unredeemable savages, Native Americans functioned more and more as templates for primal victimhood and as allies against global capitalism and fascism. I have written elsewhere about the abundant uses of Indigenous archetypes as self-serving and often patently distorted refractions of the modern self in disrepair: Ernest Hemingway's promiscuous and lazy Ojibwes, corrupted by economic exploitation and the erosion of sexual prohibitions; Willa Cather's Anasazi, vanished ancestors who failed to sustain a precapitalist idyll and whose traces on the landscape tantalize her world-weary moderns; William Faulkner's Chickasaws, who are absurd creations of the writer's imagination and containers above all for the white southerner's perceptions of dispossession and loss.

Indeed, I have written extensively about the comparative ubiquity of this phenomenon in the southern context, where defeat and dispossession triggered not just enlightenment or guilt about Indians' fate but elaborate fantasies of being and becoming Indigenous, and therefore inhabiting a nativist subjectivity that imaginatively authorized land claims and legitimacy.[16] In a 1996 Southern Focus Poll conducted by the Center for the Study of the American South at UNC, responses showed that at least 40 percent of southerners claimed descent from a Cherokee grandmother—considerably more than the

68   *The Weird South*

22 percent who proclaimed descent from a Confederate soldier, and vastly more than the 2 percent of southerners with verifiable Indigenous lineage (although the standards for recognizing ancestry are so fraught with colonial administrative politics that this is not a meaningful measure).[17] This phenomenon is pervasive in the literary culture of the South, not fading but actually intensifying throughout the twentieth century, enacting shades of apocryphal deliverance that extend far beyond the genealogical, cultural, or biological. For most of these writers, Indigenous promises fail to fulfill themselves, but they also linger uneasily—elements and signifiers of that vexed oblivion birthed by colonial capitalism, shrouded by the invisible logics of history and modernity.

It is not surprising, then, that Black southern authors like Chesnutt and Ward are drawn to the archetype of the Indigenous as an elevating facet of what might otherwise be a haunted, internalized ecological personhood—the Indian trope functioning as an authenticating device in the quest for modest reprieve. What I didn't make clear in the last chapter's discussion of Jesmyn Ward's *Sing, Unburied, Sing* is that her protagonist Jojo apparently inherits his supernatural sensitivities, which allow him to see and hear the legion ghosts saturating contemporary rural Mississippi, from his apparent Native grandfather who looks "like an Indian in the books we read in school on the Choctaw and Creek."[18] This ancestry is posed subtly as an explanation for Jojo's heightened sensitivity to the pain of others, to animal suffering, and, again, to the frail perforations between the living and the (un)dead. From a young age he already knows he can "see things that other kids didn't, like the way my teacher bit her fingernails raw, like the way she wore so much eye makeup to hide bruising from someone hitting her" (26). He visits "animals in their secret rooms in the back woods," the architecture of their environment little different from his, and when the animals speak he understands them: "it scared me to understand them, to hear them . . . But it was impossible not to hear the animals, because I looked at them and understood, instantly, and it was

The Forest 69

like looking at a sentence and understanding the words, all of it coming to me at once" (15). What is more, the relationship is reciprocal. "I knew the animals understood me, too," he says, but in the moment of its utterance the conviction is demonstrated to be pointedly useless. He has just stepped on a jagged lid of a can "rising from the earth," and, in pain, screams out to the animals or to nature or both:

> *Let me go, great tooth! Spare me!*
>   Instead, it burned and bled, and I sat on the ground in the horse's clearing and cried" until his grandfather eventually comes home. (15)

A few pages later, he hears a mosquito talking to him before it feasts on his blood (29). These moments are extraordinary because they are utterly unromantic. Taking place early in the narrative, they prepare us for a story in which the earth attacks indiscriminately, either with the jagged refuse of its abuse or with the natural hunger of all creatures to survive. Caught in the process, humans are basically unremarkable, mere hosts that provide sustenance, or victims of accidents that merit no heroic efforts to save. This is not some kind of revenge naturalism but rather a sober, humble attunement to the dynamics of our co-constitution: we can no more save the world than it can save us.

If this is the point, after all, then what *is* the point? Why do we continue to strive against the dark realities of our weird embeddedness—such a disappointing deflation of post-humanism's high hopefulness? As we have seen throughout these pages, the punctuations of succor are brief, never very encouraging (at least in the obvious ways), but nonetheless incremental—lessons for living and surviving that promise episodes of peace if not chronicles of salvation. Jojo's porousness permits him empathy, a portal to the collective consciousness that is the first order of integration, allows him to see both the horror narratives teeming in the ghost-filled forest but also opens him to the return of his incarcerated father, whom he knows to be merely "an animal on the other end of the telephone behind a fortress of concrete and bars, his voice traveling over miles of wire . . . I know what he is saying, like the birds I hear honking and flying south in the winter, like any other animal. *I'm coming home*" (30, emphasis original). The human animal, detained not for his crimes but by his nature—as Richard Wright's narrator discovers, in the patent unavailability of justice in a made world where guilt is determined by identity rather than agency. All humans are just animals, Jojo helps us understand, distanced by concrete and bars and telephone wires, and his uncanny ability is to admit them home, which is anywhere not on the other side of those fortresses. He understands all animals, even the human ones, and knows that "the wild nature" in all domesticated species will inevitably "come through," will be both its ruin and its deliverance (110).

Jojo tells one such story to soothe his baby sister, who is vomiting persistently during much of the drug-fueled trip to Parchman and back: as the sky darkens and "the forests and fields . . . turn black," he says to her,

> You see them trees over there? . . . If you look at the ground under them trees, there's a hole . . . Rabbits live in them holes. One of them is a little rabbit . . . Her name Kayla, like you. You know what she do? . . . She the best at digging holes. She dig them the deepest and the fastest. One day it was dark and a big storm come and the rabbit family's hole started filling up with water, so Kayla started digging. And digging. And digging. . . . She dug and she dug and the tunnel got longer and longer. . . . Until she popped up out the ground, and you know what? . . . . She dug all the way to our house, Kayla. . . . So when we get home, she going to be waiting for us. You want to see her? (109–10)

The parable of sorts reanimates the eviscerated rabbit in Porter's story, makes her an agent who, like so many of the protagonists we've seen in the past two chapters, keeps digging and digging variously in search of validation, liberation, escape. What Jojo's lens adds to this journey is the comfort of return, of home as a roost, and family—however tortured and

The Forest 71

torturing, however missing or incomplete—as the destination of all human stories. But we never forget how hard we fight and dig, what lessons the earth exposes along the way, what "mingled sweetness and corruption"—captured achingly here in Jojo's gentle devotion to his young sister, his offering of story despite the histories and harbingers it ineluctably evokes: "I block out the image of her in the wet earth, the size of a rabbit, digging a hole. I don't want to know that dream" (110).

Jojo's gift and burden is his comprehension of the vulnerabilities of the human, of children in inimical environments, of the many ways that humans and rabbits alike are subscendent creatures in a vast universe of interlocked energies and immense dark forests. He sees the whole for what it is and cradles the parts, sends babies to dreams and returns ghosts to the trees. He makes the forest human, and the human a forest, understanding that the boundaries will need to be endlessly fought and surmounted, over and over again. Ward's reliance on the trope of Indigeneity in all of this is neither simple nor simplistic but is a critical component of the weird personhood that exercises such a capacious energy in texts whose gravity is heavy, anchoring its characters to the sunken places of their shared haunted histories. To return to the Indigenous source of all things as an access point to a deeper, vital connectivity is a metaphor, one that serves as a prosthesis to redeem missing lines and lineages and limbs. Offered in the context of witnessing and uplifting Black experience in America, it provides a cognate mechanism to inch beyond the impasse of racialized logics that continue to imprison rather than liberate. To mark this elision in the southern context typically requires the Indian to be a trope: a vestige of Indians "in books" or the result of untraceable genealogies and never a real thing, partly because the Indigenous past in the South is perceived to be functionally inaccessible, a regional aporia accomplished by the plantation economy's first acts of obliteration. This is both true and not true, of course, depending on what we think about "truth" at the end of all

72   *The Weird South*

this—"truth" as an Anthropocenic lens for the reality we desire and hammer out of the wilderness, not for what really is, was, and will be. The very presumption of incompatibility between "real" Indian and Black American experience is one that Ward implicitly critiques even as she quietly embraces its mystifications. Tiffany Lethabo King offers a similar version of this narrowing by borrowing from "Indigenous insight into the land-body connection, or the land possessing the body, [to] offer a different way to think about and regard the Black hands that are entangled with or stained by indigo. Far from being rendered objectified bodies, they are visual reminders of the ways that the human body is always embedded in the ecologies that surround us."[19]

King follows other scholars who have been working diligently to close the perceived gap between settler-colonial and racial-capitalist experience, between that of the Indian and that of the slave, by expanding the landlocked labor matrix within which we differentially measure the socioracial identity of each. Southern history's dense overlays make such conceptual work axiomatic, if not disarmingly obvious, and it wouldn't be too aggrandizing to say that new southern studies scholars were gesturing toward this work well before Indigenous and Afropessimistic critique took up the challenge. But even here, forms of relationality founder on incommensurabilities produced by the obdurate logics of race and finance capitalism; it is impossible finally to elide the "poetics of relation" introduced by Glissant and others in the circum-Caribbean plantation complex with the landed politics and sovereignties of Indigenous thinkers like Leanne Simpson, Glen Coulthard, and others. Ecology as such seems to be the bugbear, deployed as a static trope rather than a dialectical economy of production, something the Weird South disavows and exposes with staggering candor. In the wake of Indigenous and Afropessimist logics that fundamentally but diametrically situate personhood in relation to the discrepant logics of land, labor, and identity—authorizing principles for Indigenous groups and guttering

The Forest 73

legacies for Black communities and families—critic Jared Sexton has challenged critics to imagine new forms of belonging unyoked from the specificities of place construed as property. Sexton calls for a new vocabulary of emplacement and belonging that refuses to be detained within colonialist rubrics, arguing for the "landless inhabitation of selfless existence" as a precondition for true abolition and sovereignty.[20] Similarly, in their proposal for a concept of "grounded relationalities," a group of Indigenous and ally scholars recently asked, "is there a way for land in itself to serve as an ontological condition for a different concept of the political that refuses conquest, doctrines of discovery, and the propriations of the propertied self? . . . Can land as the source of relation rather than the site of boundaries define a politics under which Indigenous sovereignty and Black reparations movements can (re)build capacities for relationality (aberrant to logics of propriation), rather than enact exclusivity or inclusion?"[21] These are powerful questions, to be sure, and they remain largely rhetorical for the moment. But if we have learned anything in these forays into the Weird South, it is that the logics of propriation do not loosen their grip without struggle or casualties and that the concept of relationality works only if the playing field (so to speak) is truly leveled. And finally, there are far more gaps to be closed than that between Indigenous and Black communities, especially if we understand their polarization to be an irrational afterbirth of the very measures we seek to upend.

Indeed, the Weird South asks us to revisit and revise two of its most essential conceits: those of land and race, apart and intertwined. Both are in many ways strategic and compulsory productions, stabilizing grounds without which our hopes for an ethical, sustainable future stagger. But, ultimately, neither the most ethically driven posthumanist thought nor the most progressive new southern studies nor the resurgent politics of Indigenous critique can have it both ways: we cannot *both* stake a proprietary claim to the salvation of radical connectedness and altered ecological futures *and* eschew the artifacts of colonial capitalism in the web—the very proprietary engines that Indigenous and Afropessimism alliances strive to disengage. In fact, we cannot do this work at all without including ourselves and our ineluctable, destructive pageants of partition—the protected species of our race and culture-bound identities—in the weird weave of all that Anthropocenic modernity has issued. We cannot continue to manufacture mythologies of return, renewal, and restoration that hinge on identity groups whose very ontology has been produced by the cognitive and biopolitical structures we now seek to escape. More fundamentally, how do we unmake the world that made us without also obliterating ourselves?

As Saidiya Hartman puts it, "The hope is that return could . . . make a victory out of defeat, and engender a new order. And the disappointment is that there is no going back . . . Loss remakes you."[22] Lisa Lowe similarly stakes a capacious claim for the "intimacies" that emerge when we read comparatively across asymmetrical cultural, discursive, and political frameworks, a method of elision that produces a fundamentally "different kind of thinking, a space of productive attention to the scene of loss."[23] Weird southern representations may be the best rendition of reality and truth that we can wrangle from the loss and the chaos, from the brutally entangled bodies, lands, and artifacts of our common making and unmaking. We can't escape the lure of the Indigenous because, frankly and finally, we can't stop yearning for that homing instinct that Ward's precocious narrator describes, that predisposition compelling all animals to return to spaces of connection, healing, and identification even in deeply traumatizing spaces of loss and wounding. Home can be many things in these processes, but most often it lures us back to the things and the places and the people that promise some aspect of self-completion, of repair, of an originary sense of being that preexists apocalypse. To invoke Hartman again, in her brilliant work on the shattering aftershocks of the global slave trade: the abiding urge for multiple generations of unsettled Black subjects is "*I shall return to my native land.* Those

The Forest 75

disbelieving in the promise and refusing to make the pledge have no choice but to avow the loss that inaugurates one's existence. It is to be bound to other promises. It is to lose your mother, always."[24]

Inauguration from loss. We cannot return the extracted baby rabbits to the womb of their mother; we are always already severed, alienated, subjected, bound, lost. Yet, like Kayla's rabbit, we never stop hunting for a means to return, to reunite, to travel back to those spaces of nourishment and rapturous relation. What stands in for such returns, in the weird southern cosmos, is the womb of earth, a place alternately nutritive and devouring, sheltering and threatful—like us, like everything, irrevocably altered by extractive demands and pressured by the weight of aboveground phantasms of community. And yet the earth exists as a reminder of what returns are possible, what frameworks of being sit in spaces, bodies, and elemental bridges between and among us.

We are left now to reckon with the concept we have been circling around delicately, in some ways, even as our conversations have been unraveling its coherence and its tyranny: that is, how do we return to the centrality of place, of location, or region—of the South itself—as a coherent identity that underlies, precedes, authorizes, identifies human life and organization? And here we disambiguate the world as we know it, that has shaped and determined us, and the weird unseen world beneath, beside, before it all. In those subterranean conceptual spaces, as we have been witnessing in these pages, and throughout the history of plantation culture not just in the South but throughout the Americas more broadly, it was precisely the entwinement of human, vegetable, animal, and inorganic forms that together produced the template for growth and industry, for carving houses and crops out of auspicious plots and materials, and for dramatizing both the necessity and the vulnerability of human bodies as simultaneously agents and casualties of this process. Land and place are not the things we own or make, in the end, but the things that imbue and transform us by turns; we can no longer plausibly say that a place belongs to us nor that we belong here, or there, or elsewhere. This is problematic, of course, because it is not the expected vocabulary of inhabitation, or of custodianship. It is certainly not the lexicon of ecological stewardship that occupies much of the environmental movement, nor is it the foundational, sovereign sensibility of the Indigenous upon whose claims to *place* settler-colonial demands effected such apocalyptical consequences and where resurgent politics remain embedded. And finally, what does this deterritorialization mean for those of us working in either Indigenous lands or southern ideological spaces, living in and identifying as one or the other? Where is the South in the landless regime of ontological reorganization and ecological and humanitarian repair? *Where are we?*

Weird southern texts present us with the ghostly hauntings of fixed locations, but they also radically exceed them. It can be a terrifying unmooring, but its practitioners ask us in some ways to give over to the dual consciousness of being here, now, and also there, someplace and sometime before and beyond the geographies that human history has carved. I want to turn now briefly to consider the enjambed Indigenous southern sensibility that might help us navigate these dialectical coordinates—weird expeditions into the forest that is, was, and will always be the landscape of our common becoming. Again, this may in some ways feel counterintuitive, given that the Native American experience, as fractured as it is within U.S. administrative politics and motivated public perceptions, occupies a more rigid place-based identification that is rivaled only distantly by other territorial attachments (such as, arguably, that of the U.S. South). As Rose Powhatan (a Pamunkey Indian from Virginia) puts it, "I'm living in a country with the curious distinction that your tribe can be changed and you can be erased from the Book of Life when you change your address. Move off the reservation and you cease to be Indian. You're dead. You never existed."[25] She is speaking on the one hand about the excessive severity of recognition politics in the U.S. South

The Forest 77

after Removal but more broadly about the nationwide measurement of Indigenous proprietorship in constant conflict with federal and state juridical perceptions and proscriptions. In response and rejoinder to such reductionist politics, Indigenous political movements (especially those attached to environmental rehabilitation programs) place emphasis on the spiritual significance of land-based sources of identity that exceed the cartographer's and capitalism's technologies. I want to acknowledge the power of these expansive cosmologies of personhood where humans derive coherence—expressed broadly via language, story, form, and meaning—in dynamic co-constitution with the cavernous striations of earth's organic and inorganic matter. Here, the Anthropocene is merely a snapshot in a dizzying expanse of deep time that, once acknowledged, unyokes us from the particularities of place and tosses us into a universe of possibility and promise. There is legion territory before and after these haunted spaces and epistemes, and hope hinges vitally on that bidirectional compass beyond the horrific caesura in between. The question is how to balance the chimera of deep time in a spectral present that vibrates with the wire ends of past and future, knit together powerfully, but which also therefore unmoors us from the compromised, constricted safety of emplacement.

I want to end with just this kind of haunted hopefulness by sharing the work of one brilliantly weird southeastern Indian: Alabama Creek poet Janet McAdams. In her poetry collections *The Island of Lost Luggage* (2000), *Feral* (2007), and *Seven Boxes for the Country After* (2016), as well as her lyrical novel *Red Weather* (2012), she returns insistently to the twisted landscapes of history, haunting, excavation, and the porous boundaries between humans, animals, and the elements that variously inspire, invent, sustain, and undo us.[26] For McAdams, the racialized Indigenous body is a sentient but ultimately imperfect vehicle—her words are "inexact" and "messy"—for carrying one's identity into the twenty-first century, for mapping its vast coordinates of loss and

78 *The Weird South*

alienation. As she puts it, the "land called 'Indigenous'" may exist only "on the map of my body."[27]

In her poetry, McAdams painfully and consistently charts that unruly body in all its locations and contacts, deterritorializing both her Indigeneity and her southernness by setting her poetry in disparate geographies and cultures that are rarely discernible or specific. The effect is distinctly and deliberately disorienting, as she interrupts the lore of tribal tradition and regional identity as privileged access points to histories that are far more immense and indiscriminately levelling. In her words, "our deepest metaphors are the furniture, language, oxygen of that other world, the 'unacknowledged' world. It is a life's work to understand them. It is the lifework of a poet to write them down."[28] The unacknowledged world—the "furniture without memories"—here and elsewhere, is legible perhaps only in the poetics of literary production. But rather than find grounds for gloom in the idea that "relation always occurs within representation,"[29] as does some Afropessimist thought, I want to suggest alongside these authors and so many Black and Indigenous critics in particular that these representational spaces may have a kind of potency we have yet to measure and harness seriously.

Feral is McAdams's collection most explicitly concerned with recovering bodies trapped within the coordinates of so-called civilization, which adheres variously in the forms of nation, region, tribe, and earth, and then plots their disaffected reentries. The blurb on the back of the book captures McAdams's driving quest: "How to understand the voice lost between forest and city, which cries, 'I am not wild, I am not human.' What lies in the need to tame ourselves and others?" Moving deftly between the poles of not-wild and not-human—the negatived interstices between antitheses—her poems hammer insistently at the origins of our impulses to domesticate and control.

In *Feral*'s final poem, "Earth My Body Is Trying to Remember," McAdams's speaker addresses "Earth" and "my

The Forest 79

body" simultaneously—enjambed in a continuous space of loss:

> We were born but born too young to remember.
> The land they took us from, the mothers' milk dried up,
> every womb a dried-up
> crackle of flesh. Earth my body
> is trying to remember.
> Child-That-Was, don't try to remember, but lean back
> into this place outside history.

McAdams reminds us that contemporary Indigenous subjects do not automatically harbor innate memory of their intimacy with land. History itself is the rupture, setting in motion a perverse settler-colonial logic of dispossession predicated precisely and paradoxically on the Indians' unitary relationship with the land. Paradoxically, to disturb that metonymy becomes a decolonizing gesture of sorts, a way of inhabiting a new geography "outside history." Once taken, the land ceases to be a nutritive subject and is rendered instead a desiccated mother. In the compressed grammar that elides "Earth" and "my body," the amnesia of the removed southeastern Indian is both invoked and shattered: the body is "trying to remember" not just earth but its own substance, a doubly foiled quest.

The Indigenous body's fatal, land-based value rises up as the bugbear, the origin of loss: "They chipped away at us, / hammered us out like gold." Sites of excavation, both the earth itself and the hollows of that earth. Much more than treasures or bodies, Indigenous subjects "were cell and stone and field, the sky: / Stars pulled down from their wandering."[30] Everything at once—a weird, expansive, webbed motion that had to be tamed. In the end—both to the poem and to the entire collection—McAdams's speaker asks her "Child-that-was" to forsake remembering, to curtail her returns to the haunted womb of the mother. In doing so, she is explicitly invoking both a fever dream of peace beyond "History" as well as its vacant potential for nourishing the woman that might be, who will and must carry forward into a vertiginous future with the memory of milk: something more than nothing, a fuel manufactured from loss but, like the empty graves and hammered-out earth-bodies, refusing its emptiness. This futility haunts not just McAdams's poetry but so much contemporary southern and Indigenous literature. The beauty of what she and others contribute is a landscape beyond loss, a time before this time, and a belief in the web that sutures together the whole without erasing the partialities—good, bad, ugly, and beautiful—of its membership.

In the aptly named "Ghost Ranch," the penultimate poem in *Feral*, McAdams's speaker and a presumed lover hiking in a canyon discover a cache of fossils. The setting of the poem is identified in the title as the real-life Ghost Ranch retreat and education center in central New Mexico, a favorite spot and subject of the painter Georgia O'Keeffe and the appealing backdrop for numerous films, including modern westerns like *Silverado* (1985), *City Slickers* (1991), *All the Pretty Horses* (2000), *No Country for Old Men* (2007), and the 2013 reprise of *Lone Ranger*. More importantly, Ghost Ranch is the site of Coelophysis Quarry, one of the most famous and oldest dinosaur mines in the world. In this extrasouthern geography of deep time, where Indigenous occupation is not an origin but merely a stage, the speaker orients us in a blistering red landscape: "land for miles and miles— / so much land," where her partner finds

> a pile of bones

> and hold[s] the pelvis up to frame a ragged disc
> of sky. Not the real sky, I thought that day,
> but blue enough to tell this story.

McAdams thus deftly reinscribes the fossil as a literary "frame"—and a "ragged," uneven one at that—as the messy matrix through which the world is made legible. The view unveils not reality, she warns, but the "story" that *is* our shared "real."

But what is *this* story in particular? The poem quietly merges a parable of postsettler exhumation with a private

The Forest 81

drama between the hiking couple, who seem to struggle for intimacy:

> We touch and circle and touch and circle
> until we only circle: cloth against cloth, skin
> not quite meeting, the way fences touch at the corners
> of nations.

The ghostly demarcations of nation and region and tribe are elided here with tangible obstacles in the quest for human contact and for fruitful union specifically—it is, after all, a pelvis bone that limns the story and uncovers the couple's freighted estrangement. Yet this is no simple lover's quarrel but an ontological crisis. "Last night you slept so quietly," she recalls,

> I put a hand to your back to make sure
> you were breathing, the other over your shoulder
> and flat against the skin between nipple
> and solar plexus: because breath may not be
> a sure enough measure. We hover
> over the animal that carved itself
> this place to rest, past molecule, atom,
> the stinging energy that drums the universe
> into being. Don't say you never felt it.
> Even the stone was pulsing. Take my hand
> if you can bear it, but let the other story go.[29]

This, the closing image of the poem, asks us to question how we "measure" life. Is it the movement of oxygen through lungs and blood, the "breath" that, in the lexicon of Pacific Islanders, is explicitly twinned with the notion of "sovereignty"? Such autonomy is not automatic in McAdams's vision, though: embodied life, community, and restorative contact come only through alienation and are rebuilt in communion with that other world via the nameless and therefore paradigmatic animal that "carved itself"—note the deliberately active verb construction—somewhere "past" and beneath the earth that we know and feel.

Like the protagonists in Porter, Chesnutt, Wright, Ward, and others that we have so briefly explored in these chapters,

82 *The Weird South*

all struggling to both seam and sever place and people, McAdams's speaker acknowledges the breach. The stone may pulse, she suggests, but it is only the human body—the emphatically present, sensual, erotic potential of the here and the now, the self and the other, urged on by the animal and the fossil but not defined or delimited by it—that gives "energy" to propel forward into an already haunted future, a new story waiting to be told. We may not be able to bear it, but we have little choice. And so we emerge from the forest now to a landscape both built and barren, the ruins of what we have made and also perhaps a stripped-down arena for discovery. We have to be willing to travel a bit to get there, to brace ourselves for exposure. In the final prose poem of McAdams's most recent collection, *Seven Boxes for the Country After* (2016), she offers a vision of a similarly stark future at a mythical inter-world waypoint: "We undress behind a screen in a small room in the space between countries. They search our pockets, tossing it all in a box marked THINGS, half full with false teeth, a tangled wig, a book losing the old skin of its binding. They search our folds, our stories . . . They take: our shoes, our pockets, the hole from the lobe of your left ear . . . They take until we are tender as babies, until we have nothing left to declare."[31]

Nothing left to declare. Is this a perverse new beginning of sorts, where one is stripped of all the prostheses of modernity, all the technologies of speech and articulation that seduce us into believing we are more than things, more than parts capable of disassembly—our stories as disposable as the things we hold dear, the things we imagine clothe, cloak, and make us? This perhaps is true rebirth, born from the haunted wombs of culture, reroutings to rawness and potentiality: "more than meat" again and always. But where *is* this country outside and after history? In the speculative worlds of weirdness, we find grace and novelty, beauty and absurdity and greed for something other than—but inclusive of—the "THINGS" that tether and create us: who we are and what we own functioning together, all impermanent, detachable, vulnerable to loss. To have "nothing left to declare" is to be without a passport, one that so deeply imprints and supplements the body; there is mourning in the loss, a stunned silence, but also, perhaps, a tender, weird hope for new stories, alliances, stitches, and skins.

Notes

Preface

1. Timothy Morton, "Buddaphobia: Nothingness and the Fear of Things," in *Nothing: Three Inquiries in Buddhism*, by Marcus Boon, Eric Cazdyn, and Timothy Morton (Chicago: The University of Chicago Press, 2015), 185–266. 250.

Chapter 1. The Grave

1. Katherine Anne Porter, "The Grave," *Virginia Quarterly Review* 11, no. 2 (1935): 183. Subsequent quotations from this text are cited parenthetically.

2. See, for instance, Jennifer Greeson's *Our South: Geographic Fantasy and the Rise of National Literature* (Cambridge: Harvard University Press, 2010).

3. Elsewhere, I have developed the concept of "Weird Indigeneity" to likewise identify the contributions of Indigenous writers to apprehending a tangled biosphere, but without surrendering to the exclusive or essential politics of difference. Weird Indigeneity, I argue, "need not—in fact, it cannot—be 'Indigenous' in the ways and terms we come to define it. . . . [S]olidifying any cultural group—particularly a pan-tribal, motley, global aggregate such as that bundled awkwardly in the modern signifier of 'Indigenous'—only enables the pernicious politics of settler-colonial and capitalist logics that depend on facile divisions." "Indigeneity: Posthumanist Fantasy and Weird Reality," in *The Cambridge Companion to Animals and Literature*, ed. Derek Ryan (Cambridge: Cambridge University Press, 2023), 220–35.

4. Paraphrased on the Penguin Random House page, "So You Want to Read Weird Fiction: Here's Where to Start": https://www.penguinrandomhouse.com/the-read-down/want-read-weird-fiction-heres-start/.

5. Morton, Timothy, "Weird Embodiment," in *Sentient Performativities of Embodiment: Thinking Alongside the Human*, ed. Lynette Hunter, Elisabeth Krimmer, and Peter Lichtenfels (Lanham: Lexington Books, 2016), 20.

6. Morton, *Dark Ecology* (New York: Columbia University Press, 2016), 7.

7. Morton, "Weird Embodiment," 29.

8. Roy Scranton. *Learning to Die in the Anthropocene: Reflections on the End of a Civilization* (San Francisco, CA: City Lights Books, 2015).

9. See, for instance, Rob Nixon's pivotal *Slow Violence and the Environmentalism of the Poor* (Cambridge, Mass.: Harvard University Press, 2011), which exposes the accretive, global impacts of racial capitalist "progress" particularly and acutely on the marginalized, displaced, and poor. Similarly, Kathryn Yusoff, in both *A Billion Black Anthropocenes or None* (Minneapolis: University of Minnesota Press, 2019) as well as a forthcoming book on geology and race, deftly articulates the coeval constructions of Anthropocenic time and geological thinking with the racialized subjects produced within their extractive economies.

10. Tiffany Lethabo King, Jenell Navarro, and Andrea Smith, eds., *Otherwise Worlds: Against Settler Colonialism and Anti-Blackness* (Durham: Duke University Press, 2020).

11. Yusoff, *A Billion Black Anthropocenes*.

12. Yusoff.

13. Yusoff.

14. Timothy Morton, *Humankind: Solidarity with Non-human People* (Brooklyn, N.Y.: Verso, 2017), 118. Emphasis mine.

15. And it does: in the unfolding conversations about Anthropocene diagnosis and repair, Indigenous knowledge is routinely invoked as uniquely positioned and equipped to shepherd the latter. However, many Indigenous thinkers have objected to the cooptation of their knowledge systems, frequently without citation or specificity. See especially Zoe Todd, "Indigenizing the Anthropocene", in Heather Davis and Etienne Turpin, eds., *Art in the Anthropocene: Encounters Among Aesthetics, Politics, Environments and Epistemologies* (London: Open Humanities Press, 2015), pp. 241–54; "An Indigenous feminist's take on the ontological turn: 'Ontology' is just another word for colonialism", *Journal of His-*

torical Sociology (2016), vol. 29, no. 1, pp. 4-22; and Kyle Whyte, "Indigenous Science (Fiction) for the Anthropocene: Ancestral Dystopias and Fantasies of Climate Change Crises," *Environment and Planning. Nature and Space* 1, no. 1–2 (2018): 224–42. doi:10.1177/2514848618777621 and "Too Late for Indigenous Climate Justice: Ecological and Relational Tipping Points," *Wiley Interdisciplinary Reviews. Climate Change* 11, no. 1 (2020): e603-n/a. doi:10.1002/wcc.603.

16. Timothy Morton, *Hyperobjects: Philosophy and Ecology after the End of the World* (Minneapolis: University of Minnesota Press, 2013), 139.

17. Morton, *Hyperobjects*, 62.

18. Morton, *Hyperobjects*, 66.

19. Avery Gordon, *Ghostly Matters: Haunting and the Sociological Imagination* (Minneapolis: University of Minnesota Press, 2008).

20. Gordon, 25.

21. Gordon, 27.

22. Interview with Nicholas Korody, "Timothy Morton on haunted architecture, dark ecology, and other objects," Archinect, March 11, 2016, https://archinect.com/features/article/149934079/timothy-morton-on-haunted-architecture-dark-ecology-and-other-objects.

23. I have written elsewhere about southern writers' complex and longstanding use of Indigenous histories and tropes to capture the region's own experience of dispossession. See in particular my *Reconstructing the Native South: American Indian Literature and the Lost Cause* (Athens: University of Georgia Press, 2012) and *The Indian in American Southern Literature* (Cambridge: Cambridge University Press, 2020).

24. According to the Oxford English Dictionary, "ecstasy" describes the experience of being "beside oneself," often in a "state of rapture in which the body was supposed to become incapable of sensation, while the soul was engaged in the contemplation of divine things." Oxford English Dictionary, s.v. "ecstasy (n.), sense 3.b," December 2023, https://doi.org/10.1093/OED/3430999869.

25. James William Johnson, "Another Look at Katherine Anne Porter," *Virginia Quarterly Review* 36, no. 4 (Fall, 1960): 609–10, https://www.proquest.com/scholarly-journals/another-look-at-katherine-anne-porter/docview/1291794714/se-2.

Notes to Pages 10–21   87

26. Patricia Yaeger, "Ghosts and Shattered Bodies, or What Does It Mean to Still Be Haunted by Southern Literature?" *South Central Review* 22, no. 1 (Spring 2005): 90.

27. Yaeger, 96.

28. Morton, *Hyperobjects*, 69.

29. Morton, *Dark Ecology*, 6.

30. Yaeger, "Ghosts and Shattered Bodies," 97.

31. Benjamin Boysen, "The Embarrassment of Being Human: A Critique of New Materialism and Object-Oriented Ontology," *Orbis Litterarum* 73 (2018): 229.

32. Patricia Yaeger, *Dirt and Desire: Reconstructing Southern Women's Writing, 1930–1990* (Chicago: University of Chicago Press, 2000), 20.

33. Mary Titus, *The Ambivalent Art of Katherine Anne Porter* (Athens: University of Georgia Press, 2005), 119.

34. The story's central events take place in 1903.

35. In a search for "mind's eye," the *Oxford English Dictionary* lists just two occurrences that employ with the phrase the preposition "before" versus thirty-eight that use the preposition "in" or "of" (oed.com, accessed March 12, 2024).

36. In a reading of Willa Cather's novel *My Ántonia*, and its eruptions of southern plantation trauma in unexpected remove (the Nebraska prairie on the early twentieth-century western frontier), Matthews builds on Žižek's concept of cultural fetishism, a variation on the familiar Marxian scheme, to explain these operations: "the people know very well how things really are, but still they are doing it as if they did not." Quoted in "Willa Cather and the Burden of Southern History," *Philological Quarterly* 90, nos. 2/3 (2011): 137–65.

37. Sarah Robertson, "Accessing Blood-Knowledge in Katherine Anne Porter's 'The Old Order,'" *Mississippi Quarterly* 62, no. 2 (2009): 249, http://www.jstor.org/stable/26476737.

38. Mary Titus, "'Mingled Sweetness and Corruption': Katherine Anne Porter's 'The Fig Tree' and 'The Grave,'" *South Atlantic Review* 53, no. 2 (1988): 111–25.

39. Katherine Anne Porter, "The Fig Tree," in *The Collected Stories of Katherine Anne Porter* (New York: New American Library, 1970), 361.

Chapter 2. The Trees

1. Avery Gordon, *Ghostly Matters: Haunting and the Sociological Imagination* (Minneapolis: University of Minnesota Press, 2008), 3.

2. See, for instance, Annie Olaloku-Teriba, "Afro-Pessimism and the (Un)Logic of Anti-Blackness," *Historical Materialism* 26, no. 2 (2018): 108–9.

3. Tiana Clark, "Broken Sestina Reaching for Black Joy," in *Inheritance* series, *The Atlantic*, September 17, 2021, https://www.theatlantic.com/books/archive/2021/09/poem-tiana-clark-broken-sestina-reaching-black-joy/619980/.

4. Monique Allewaert, *Ariel's Ecology Plantations, Personhood, and Colonialism in the American Tropics* (Minneapolis: University of Minnesota Press, 2013), 1.

5. Allewaert, 2.

6. Zakiyyah Iman Jackson, *Becoming Human: Matter and Meaning in an Antiblack World* (New York: New York University Press, 2021), 1.

7. The story was not originally included in the 1899 edition of *The Conjure Woman and Other Tales* but was included later by Richard Brodhead in the 1993 repackaging of the collection. To many critics, Karen Carmean explains, it is "thematically of a whole with all of the conjure tales." Karen Carmean, "Charles Chesnutt: Crossing the Colour Line," *Canadian Review of American Studies* 25, no. 2 (1995): 101.

8. Slavoj Žižek, *Absolute Recoil: Towards a New Foundation of Dialectic Materialism* (London, UK: Verso, 2015), 8n8.

9. Hurston uses this phrase in her seven-page proposal to engage in a WPA recording effort throughout the state of Florida, which she delineates as one of the most diverse incubators of diasporic cultures in the nation. See Zora Neale Hurston, *Proposed Recording Expedition into the Floridas*, May 1939, Manuscript/Mixed Material, Library of Congress, https://www.loc.gov/item/flwpa000213/.

10. Eduoard Glissant, *The Poetics of Relation*, trans. Betsy Wing (Ann Arbor: University of Michigan Press, 1997), 6.

11. Glissant, 9.

12. Gilles Deleuze and Félix Guattari, *Kafka: Toward a Minor*

Literature. (Minneapolis: University of Minnesota Press, 1986), 83.

13. Susan Scott Parrish attends to these myriad alternative and biotic expressions and texts, with particular focus on early American archives, in order to "help to dissipate our bookish tendency to see literacy as the defining threshold to personhood in the period, and . . . give examples to scholars of later periods in how to include environmental and biological history in their interdisciplinary tool kit." Parrish, "Rummaging/In and Out of Holds," *Early American Literature* 45, no. 2 (2010): 271.

14. Indeed, a note included in the 2021 edition indicates that an editor found "unbearable" the protagonist's brutal treatment by the police. "Note on the Texts," in Richard Wright, *The Man Who Lived Underground* (New York: Harper Perennial, 2021), 224. Subsequent references to this text will be cited parenthetically. As poet Reginald Dwayne Betts observed in a *New York Times* review, "the restored novel feels wearily descriptive of far too many moments in contemporary America." Betts, "Richard Wright's Newly Restored Novel Is a Tale for Today," *New York Times*, April 20, 2021, https://www.nytimes.com/2021/04/20/books/review/richard -wright-man-who-lived-underground.html.

15. David Bradley, "Introduction," to Richard Wright, *12 Million Black Voices* (New York: Basic Books, 2008), xix. "Teeming" is Wright's word identifying "the black millions who endured the physical and spiritual ravages of serfdom" and who fled the South during the 1930s and the collapse of the cotton economy. "Preface" to *12 Million Black Voices*, xxi.

16. Wright, *12 Million Black Voices*, 10–11.

17. Wright, 49.

18. Wright, 146, 147.

19. Paula Rabinowitz, "'Between the Outhouse and the Garbage Dump': Locating Collapse in Depression Literature," *American Literary History* 23, no. 1 (Spring 2011): 33.

20. Wright, *Man Who Lived Underground*, 5.

21. In "Memories of my Grandmother," the essay written to accompany the novel and published along with it in the 2021 edition, he declared that nothing he wrote before or after "stemmed more from sheer inspiration . . . from my own personal background, reading, experiences, and feelings." Wright, *Man Who Lived Underground*, 163.

22. Wright, *Man Who Lived Underground*, 223.

23. Wright, 169.

24. Colleen Glenney Boggs, "*American Hunger* vs. *America Eats*: Richard Wright and the Racial Politics of Lifestyle Writing," *American Literary History* 35, no. 4 (2023): 1651.

25. Boggs, "*American Hunger* vs. *America Eats*," 1647.

26. Imani Perry, "What Richard Wright Knew," *The Atlantic*, June 1, 2021, 84.

27. Wright, *Man Who Lived Underground*, 159.

28. Jesmyn Ward, *Sing, Unburied, Sing: A Novel* (New York: Scribner, 2017). Subsequent quotations from this text are cited parenthetically.

29. I am deliberately conjuring Jordan Peele's concept from his acclaimed racial horror film *Get Out* (2017), where "the sunken place" functions as postracial abyss, the underground space in a plantation pantomime lifted out of southern history and into a context of liberal ideologies in upstate New York, where the worst horrors and brutal physical cooptations take place in the name of "progress."

Chapter 3. The Forest

1. Oxford English Dictionary, s.v. "white-knuckle (v.)," June 2024, https://doi.org/10.1093/OED/7430070202.

2. Timothy Morton, *Humankind: Solidarity with Nonhuman People* (London: Verso, 2017), 1.

3. This is the premise of Patricia Stuelke's study *The Ruse of Repair: U.S. Neoliberal Empire and the Turn from Critique* (Durham: Duke University Press, 2021). Stuelke argues that the reparative modes of much neoliberal critique reproduce—and are, in fact, produced by—U.S. modes of imperial, colonial, and military violence.

4. David Graeber, "Radical Alterity Is Just Another Way of Saying 'Reality': A Reply to Eduardo Viveiros de Castro," *HAU Journal of Ethnographic Theory* 5, no. 2 (2015): 22.

5. Quoted in Jaskiram Dhillon, "Indigenous Resurgence, Decolonization, and Movements for Environmental Justice," introduction to *Indigenous Resurgence: Decolonization and Movements for Environmental Justice*, ed. Jaskiram Dhillon (New York: Berghahn, 2022), 7.

6. Elaine Gan, Anna Tsing, Heather Swanson, and Nils Bubandt, "Introduction: Haunted Landscapes of The Anthropocene," In *Arts*

Notes to Pages 54–65   91

of Living on a Damaged Planet (University of Minnesota Press, 2017), 1–14; Donna J. Haraway, *Staying with the Trouble: Making Kin in the Chthulucene* (Duke University Press, 2016); Deborah Bird Rose, "Multispecies Knots of Ethical Time." *Environmental Philosophy* 9, no. 1 (2012): 127–40, 135. http://www.jstor.org/stable/26169399; David Farrier, *Anthropocene Poetics: Deep Time, Sacrifice Zones, and Extinction* (Minneapolis; University of Minnesota Press, 2019), especially chapter 2, pp. 51–88; Morton, *Humankind*, 1.

7. See especially Sarah Hunt, "Ontologies of Indigeneity: The Politics of Embodying a Concept," *Cultural Geographies* 21, no. 1 (2014): 27–32. doi:10.1177/1474474013500226 and Zoe Todd, "Indigenizing the Anthropocene", in Heather Davis and Etienne Turpin, eds., *Art in the Anthropocene: Encounters Among Aesthetics, Politics, Environments and Epistemologies* (London: Open Humanities Press, 2015), pp. 241–54

8. Rebekah Sheldon, *The Child to Come: Life after the Human Catastrophe* (University of Minnesota Press, 2016), vii.

9. More about the film is available at the International Film Festival Rotterdam website, https://iffr.com/en/2020/films/the-mermaids-or-aiden-in-wonderland. The film has been lauded as "a powerful intervention in contemporary debates about the future present of climate change, extractive capitalism, and industrial toxicity from the point of view of Indigenous worlds."

10. As Timothy Morton puts it in *Humankind: Solidarity with Non-human People* (Brooklyn, N.Y.: Verso, 2017), scholars' legitimate fears of appropriating non-Western cultural knowledge "miss the target because they rely on an idea of the incommensurability of cultures," which is itself "a symptom of the very imperialism from which one is trying to rescue thinking by departing from strong correlationist orthodoxy. How ironic is that?" (12)

11. Stuart Hall, "Cultural Identity and Diaspora," in *Theorizing Diaspora: A Reader*, ed. Jana Evans Braziel and Anita Mannur (Malden, Mass.: Blackwell, 2003), 245.

12. Annie Olaloku-Teriba, "Afro-Pessimism and the (Un)Logic of Anti-Blackness," *Historical Materialism* 26, no. 2 (2018): 108–9.

13. For more on the expanded purview of these new economic histories, see Kenneth Lipartito, "Reassembling the Economic: New Departures in Historical Materialism," *American Historical Review* 121, no. 1 (2016): 101–39. Lipartito applauds the ways that sussing

"the interconnections between material and symbolic life is at the heart of the new literature . . . bring[ing] the economic back into the larger narratives of history" (101). Lipartito notes that much of this reorientation resulted from historians' forays into cultural anthropology and literary theory and calls for continued efforts to eliminate "the walls between economic, social, and cultural history" (102).

14. For a wide-ranging exploration of the affinities between capitalism and spectrality, see Joseph Vogl, *The Specter of Capital*, trans. Joachim Redner and Robert Savage (Stanford, Calif.: Stanford University Press, 2015).

15. See, for instance, Alan Trachtenberg's *Shades of Hiawatha* (New York: Hill and Wang, 2004), which argues for the seductive applications of the Native American experience to the development of a national identity, particularly for immigrants in the early twentieth century.

16. See in particular Melanie Benson Taylor, *Reconstructing the Native South : American Indian Literature and the Lost Cause* (Athens: University of Georgia Press, 2011) and *The Indian in American Southern Literature* (Cambridge: Cambridge University Press, 2020).

17. John Shelton Reed, "The Cherokee Princess in the Family Tree" *Southern Cultures* 3, no. 1 (1997): 111–13. doi:10.1353/scu.1997.0057.

18. Jesmyn Ward, *Sing, Unburied, Sing: A Novel* (New York: Scribner, 2017), 12. Subsequent quotations from this text are cited parenthetically.

19. Tiffany Lethabo King, *The Black Shoals: Offshore Formations of Black and Native Studies* (Durham: Duke University Press, 2019), 114.

20. Jared Sexton, "The *Vel* of Slavery: Tracking the Figure of the Unsovereign," *Critical Sociology* 42, nos. 4/5 (2016): 583–97.

21. Jodi A. Byrd, Alyosha Goldstein, Jodi Melamed, and Chandan Reddy, "Predatory Value: Economies of Dispossession and Disturbed Relationalities," *Social Text* 36, no. 2 (2018): 11.

22. Saidiya V. Hartman, *Lose Your Mother: A Journey along the Atlantic Slave Route* (New York: Farrar, Straus and Giroux, 2007), 100.

23. Lisa Lowe, *The Intimacies of Four Continents* (Durham: Duke University Press, 2015), 41. Doi:10.1515/9780822375647.

24. Hartman, *Lose Your Mother*, 100.

25. Rose Powhatan, "Surviving Document Genocide," *The People Who Stayed: Southeastern Indian Writing after Removal*, ed. Geary Hobson, Janet McAdams, and Kathryn Walkiewicz (Norman: University of Oklahoma Press, 2010), 23–24.

26. Janet McAdams, *The Island of Lost Luggage* (Tucson: University of Arizona Press, 2000); *Feral* (Great Wilbraham, Cambridge, UK: Salt Publishing, 2007); *Seven Boxes for the Country After* (Kent, Ohio: Kent State University Press, 2016); and *Red Weather* (Tucson: University of Arizona Press, 2012).

27. Janet McAdams, "From *Betty Creek*: Writing the Indigenous Deep South," in *The People Who Stayed: Southeastern Indian Writing after Removal*, ed. Geary Hobson, Janet McAdams, and Kathryn Walkiewicz (Norman: University of Oklahoma Press, 2010), 256.

28. McAdams, "From *Betty Creek*," 256.

29. Frank B. Wilderson, *Afropessimism* (New York, N.Y.: Liveright Publishing Corporation, 2020), 315.

30. Janet McAdams, "Earth My Body Is Trying to Remember," in *Feral* (Norfolk, UK: Salt Publishing, 2007), 76.

31. Janet McAdams, *Seven Boxes for the Country After* (Kent, Ohio: Kent State University Press, 2016), Kindle edition.

Index

African American literature, 34; Chesnutt, 36–43; Hurston, 45; Ward, 69–72; Wright, 48–58, 67–68, 71, 90n15, 90n21

African American subjects. *See* Black and brown subjects

Afropessimism, 13, 34, 35, 39, 73, 75

Aiden in Wonderland, The Mermaids, or (Povinelli), 66, 92n9

Allewaert, Monique, 35, 44

alterity. *See* others and otherness

American Hunger (Wright), 48

archetypes and stereotypes. *See* stereotypes and archetypes

Betts, Reginald Dwayne, 90n14

Black American literature. *See* African American literature

Black and brown subjects, 7, 11, 13–14, 27, 33–34, 48, 64; in "The Dumb Witness," 38–43; in Wright's oeuvre, 48–58

Black culture, 45. *See also* African American literature

Black labor and laborers, 10, 26, 33, 49, 51

Boggs, Colleen Glenney, 54

Boysen, Benjamin, 22–23

Bradley, David, 49

Bull, Malcolm, 26

Cather, Willa, 68; *My Ántonia*, 88n36

"Cherokee grandmother" claims, 68–69

Chesnutt, Charles W., 69; "The Dumb Witness," 36–43, 44

Clark, Tiana, 34

climate change and climate disaster, xii, xvi, 5, 66

correlationism, 3, 10, 33, 64, 92n10

COVID-19 pandemic, xvi, 63

decomposition, 32, 35, 43, 44, 46

Deleuze, Gilles, 47

deterritorialization, 77, 79

dispossession, 7, 13, 15, 16, 68, 80

"Dumb Witness, The" (Chesnutt), 36–43, 44

"Earth My Body Is Trying to Remember" (McAdams), 79–81

Farrier, David, 65

Faulkner, William: *Go Down Moses*, 26; Indigenous subjects, 68

Feral (McAdams), 78, 79, 81
"Fig Tree, The" (Porter), 28–29, 33
furniture, 33, 34, 44; as metaphor, 32, 40–41, 79

Gan, Elaine, 65
Get Out (Peele), 91n29
"Ghost Ranch" (McAdams), 81–82
ghosts. *See* haunting
"Ghosts and Shattered Bodies" (Yaeger), 14, 21–22
Glissant, Édouard, 45–46; "poetics of relation," 73
Go Down Moses (Faulkner), 26
Gordon, Avery, 11, 32
Graeber, David, 64
"Grave, The" (Porter), 1, 14–28, 31, 36
Guattari, Félix, 47

Hall, Stuart, 66
Haraway, Donna, 14, 65
Harman, Graham, 2–3, 65
Hartman, Saidiya, 75–76
haunting, 11–12, 14, 32, 59–60, 77, 78
Heidegger, Martin, 51
Hemingway, Ernest, 68
Holocaust, Jewish, 43
Hunt, Sarah, 65
Hurricane Ian, xi–xii
Hurston, Zora Neale, 45

Ian, Hurricane, xi–xii
Indigeneity and Indigenous identity, 8, 9, 22, 43, 45, 62–66, 68–70, 72–75; "Cherokee grandmother" claims, 68–69; Powhatan

on, 77; "Weird Indigeneity," 8, 62–63, 85n3
Indigenous culture, 8, 9, 22, 44, 45, 47; literature, 47, 78–84
Indigenous removal, 16
Indigenous sovereignty, 73, 74, 77, 82
Indigenous subjects, 13–14, 25, 43, 68, 69–70, 72–73, 78, 80

Jackson, Zakiyyah Iman, 35
Jewish Holocaust, 43
Johnson, James William, 20–21
Joon-hoo, Bong, 66

King, Tiffany Lethabo, 73

"Letter on Humanism" (Heidegger), 51
Lipartito, Kenneth, 92–93n13
Lovecraft, H. P., 2–3, 5
Lowe, Lisa, 75

Man Who Lived Underground, The (Wright), 48, 50–58, 67–68, 71, 90n21
Matthews, John T., 24, 88n36
McAdams, Janet, 78–84; "Earth My Body Is Trying to Remember," 79–81; *Feral*, 78, 79, 81; "Ghost Ranch," 81–82; *Seven Boxes for the Country After*, 83
Mermaids, or Aiden in Wonderland, The (Povinelli), 66, 92n9
Michaels, Walter Benn, 68
Möbius strip metaphor, xv–xvi, xvii, 4, 11, 36

Morrison, Toni, 32
Morton, Timothy, 3–5, 8–12, 21–22, 33, 63, 64, 65, 92n10; on etymology of "weird," xv
My Ántonia (Cather), 88n36

Native American culture. *See* Indigenous culture
Native American identity. *See* Indigeneity and Indigenous identity
Native American removal, 16
Native American sovereignty. *See* Indigenous sovereignty
Native American subjects. *See* Indigenous subjects
nativism, 16, 68
nihilism, 6, 58

Olaloku-Teriba, Annie, 67
Old Order, The (Porter), 26, 27, 28–29
others and otherness, 3, 7, 10, 11, 13, 34–35; African American, 17; Indigenous, 64

Parrish, Susan Scott, 90n13
Peele, Jordan, 91n29
Perry, Imani, 55
plantations, 33, 35, 36, 46, 62, 72, 76; in fiction, 26, 36–43, 88n36; in films, 91n29; in *12 Million Black Voices*, 49, 51
Porter, Katherine Anne: biographical details, 24; "The Fig Tree," 28–29, 33; "The Grave," 1, 14–29, 31, 36; *The Old Order*, 26, 27, 28–29

Povinelli, Elizabeth, 65; *The Mermaids*, 66, 92n9
Powhatan, Rose, 77

Rabinowitz, Paula, 50
race and racialization, 7, 8, 11, 12, 13, 22, 36, 44; Indigenous subjects, 78; skin color, 36, 38. *See also* Black and brown subjects
Robertson, Sarah, 26
Rose, Deborah Bird, 65
Roy, Arundhati, 65

science fiction and speculative fiction, 47, 66
Scranton, Roy, 6
Seven Boxes for the Country After (McAdams), 83
Sexton, Jared, 74
Sing, Unburied, Sing (Ward), 58–60, 61, 69–72, 75
skin color, 36, 38
slavery, 10, 33, 35–36, 44, 62, 73; in "The Dumb Witness," 36, 41; formerly enslaved people in fiction, 38–43; in "The Grave," 27; hidden in plain sight, 24; reparations, 74; in *12 Million Black Voices*, 48, 49, 51
slave trade, 75; slave ship as "womb abyss," 45
Snowpiercer (Joon-hoo), 66
sovereignty, Indigenous. *See* Indigenous sovereignty
stereotypes and archetypes: of Indigenous people, 68, 69–70; racial, 54; southern, 2

Titus, Mary, 26–27
Todd, Zoe, 65

Index 97

12 *Million Black Voices*
(Wright), 48–49, 50, 51,
90n15

Ward, Jesmyn, 69; *Sing,
Unburied, Sing,* 58–60, 61,
69–72, 75
"weird," etymology of, xv
"Weird Indigeneity," 8, 62–63,
85n3
Whyte, Kyle, 66
wilderness, 18, 58, 68, 73
Wilderson, Frank. *See*
Afropessimism
"womb abyss," slave ship as
(Glissant), 45

women and girls, repression of,
17, 19–20, 39
Wright, Richard: *American
Hunger,* 48; *The Man Who
Lived Underground,* 48,
50–58, 67–68, 71, 90n21;
12 *Million Black Voices,*
48–49, 50, 51, 90n15

Yaeger, Patricia, 23; "Ghosts
and Shattered Bodies," 14,
21–22
Yusoff, Kathryn, 7

Žižek, Slavoj, 43, 88n36

Selected books from the Mercer University Lamar Memorial Lectures

Remapping Southern Literature:
Contemporary Southern Writers and the West
Robert H. Brinkmeyer Jr.

A Web of Words: The Great Dialogue of Southern Literature
Richard Gray

Remembering Medgar Evers:
Writing the Long Civil Rights Movement
Minrose Gwin

The Power of the Porch: The Storyteller's Craft in
Zora Neale Hurston, Gloria Naylor, and Randall Kenan
Trudier Harris

The Southern Writer in the Postmodern World
Fred Hobson

A Late Encounter with the Civil War
Michael Kreyling

The North of the South: The Natural World and the National Im-
aginary in the Literature of the Upper South
Barbara Ladd

Daughters of Time: Creating Woman's Voice in Southern Story
Lucinda H. MacKethan

Hidden in Plain Sight: Slave Capitalism in
Poe, Hawthorne, and Joel Chandler Harris
John T. Matthews

The Zombie Memes of Dixie
Scott Romine

*The Hammers of Creation: Folk Culture in
Modern African-American Fiction*
Eric J. Sundquist

*The Literary Percys: Family History, Gender,
and the Southern Imagination*
Bertram Wyatt-Brown

Printed in the United States
by Baker & Taylor Publisher Services